Kingdom Moments

Kingdom Moments

Hearing and responding to the Voice of God

Wendell T. Robinson

XULON PRESS

Xulon Press
2301 Lucien Way #415
Maitland, FL 32751
407.339.4217
www.xulonpress.com

Paperback ISBN-13: 9781662857577
Ebook ISBN-13: 9781662857584

Endorsements

It is this *relational* aspect of Wendell's faith that seems to permeate everything he says and does. It is this unwavering focus on "relationship" that lies at the heart of *Kingdom Moments*. Again and again, readers are urged to prioritize, above all else, their personal relationships with the Father, Son, and Holy Spirit.

—Joseph Anfuso
Author & Founder, Forward Edge International

Dedication

To the sweet Holy Spirit who perched on my shoulder speaking to me step by step what to do as a young Jesus follower and has done so ever since.

To my beloved wife Lisa Robinson who followed me as I followed Jesus. I'm thankful that as young believers we were taught together to hear and obey the voice of the Holy Spirit.

To my three sons, Caleb, Josiah, and Eli who are three of the strongest young men I know. Dad will always love you for who you are.

To all those who inspired me to live in a "free fall" for Jesus I dedicate this work to you.

Acknowledgments

Dr. James and Lynetta Martin who took us in when we were young Jesus followers as their own children and modeled the Jesus life.

Dr. Virgil and Martha Amos who opened the world of global missions and encouraged us to die so that Christ could live in us.

Pastor Ron and Debbie Bronski true Jesus followers called to the least, the lost and the unlovely. Thank you for showing us what a laid down life for Jesus looks like.

Pastors Rolando and Vivian Cruz who discipled and adopted us as their Puerto Rican children, "pura cepa." Gracias por modelar la vida sobrenatural de Cristo.

Teresa Liebscher who through faith and obedience Father God used as a conduit to bring prophetic revelation and inspiration to our lives.

Genevieve and Manfred Robinson A.KA. Mom and Dad who love me and Lisa unconditionally, always encouraging us to go for our dreams.

Table of Contents

Foreword

L et me start by saying, I believe devotionals should be written only by those with long track records of deep devotion to Christ, sacrificial service of others, and a broad range of kingdom-advancing experience. The man who created the devotional you hold in your hands meets all of these criteria. Which is why I agreed to write this foreword.

I first met Wendell Robinson in 2016 when he inquired about a job at the international relief and development organization I was then leading. At the time, Wendell was working for a similar organization in Atlanta, but sensed God leading him to relocate with his family to the Portland, Oregon area, his hometown, where my organization is based. I ended up offering Wendell the job, and for more than 3 years we were both coworkers and personal friends.

As the years passed, I grew in my love and respect for Wendell. Not only was he a seasoned missionary and community-development practitioner, he was also a passionate follower of Jesus, with an infectious love for God and others. It was this *relational* aspect of Wendell's faith that seemed to permeate everything he said and did.

It is this unwavering focus on "relationship" that lies at the heart of *Kingdom Moments*. Again and again, readers are urged to prioritize, above all else, their personal relationships with the Father, Son, and Holy Spirit. Repeated exhortations in the devotional include: Spend time in God's presence! Learn to hear God's voice! Do whatever the Spirit directs, without hesitating! And while I've been following Jesus for almost 50 years, I can honestly say that *Kingdom Moments* inspired me afresh to do all of these things.

A unique feature of *Kingdom Moments* is its "Reflection Questions." These questions are designed to help readers apply what they read to their actual lives. "Don't merely listen to the word," James 1:22 warns, "and so deceive yourselves. *Do* what it says." Which is precisely what these questions will help you to do.

As I said at the outset, devotionals should only be written by followers of Jesus who meet certain criteria. I can assure you, as you make your way through this devotional, you'll be receiving from a man who loves Jesus with all his heart, loves others well, and knows what it takes to advance God's Kingdom—here in the U.S., and around the world. Be blessed!

—Joseph Anfuso
Founder, Forward Edge International

Introduction:
HEAR GOD'S VOICE DAILY

I n 2002, we were part of a tremendous ministry and move of God while living as missionaries in Ponce, Puerto Rico. During that season, the leadership of the church emphasized the importance of learning to hear the voice of God. Kingdom moments began with our journey in refining and developing our ability to hear the voice of God. We were challenged to rise up every morning like David in Psalms 63:1 when he said, *"O God, You are my God; Early will I seek You; My soul thirsts for You; My flesh longs for You In a dry and thirsty land Where there is no water"* and ask the Lord to speak to us from His Word. Once we heard from the Lord, we were instructed to journal what He said. Accompanying our daily rising to hear the voice of God were consistent prayer and fasting.

Focusing intently on hearing God speak on a regular basis wasn't something we were particularly used to doing. Before long we could hear Him speak. Sometimes it would be as clear as a verse from the scriptures. Other times it would come in the form of a phrase that I would have to search for to find the specific text in scripture. Once we had the scripture, the next step was to write down what we heard God saying. During the process I can remember thinking to myself, "Can I do this every day?" "Will there be times I get up to meet God and hear nothing?" Without fail, daily God had something to say. As a side note for anyone who wants to practice hearing from God, I recommend buying a journal to jot down the things He says to you. We would use a calendar journal. Each page would have the day of the month with note lines to write. For example, Monday January 1, then several lines to make notes on that day. The next page would say Tuesday January 2 and so on. To this day I have several calendar journals documenting my journey with Father God.

Several years later, I was sitting in my office during my morning devotional time. At the time, my three sons were living in the state of

Georgia. We were living in Washington State. I felt the urge to encourage them in the Word, so I said to the Lord, "I want to send them a word from You every day, not from a devotional, but from You." "Give me a word daily as you did when we lived in Puerto Rico." Without fail the Lord began giving me something from His Word every single day. I'd rise in the morning. God would speak. I'd write down the scripture and all He had to say. Then I'd send the word to my boys via text message. This went on for quite some time.

When the global pandemic hit in our state we were under a "shelter-in-place" order by the Governor. As many experienced, we could only leave our homes for the essentials: gas, banking, and visits to the grocery store. Many churches had to close their doors for in-person services. We were no longer permitted to gather on Sundays in-person. With this type of protocol in place, I had to find a different way to encourage and disciple my congregation.

I began talking to God once again about giving me a word that I could write down and share with my congregation on a regular basis during the pandemic. I not only wanted to encourage them, I wanted to invite them with me to explore God's vast Kingdom. I wanted them to know His thoughts from the perspective of the Kingdom of Heaven. I wanted to invite them to encounter the living God for themselves. One of my favorite versus from the Bible is found in what has been referred to as the Lord's Prayer: *"Your Kingdom come, your will be done on earth as it is in Heaven," Matthew 6:10.* Each morning I met the Lord in my secret place to receive what I called "Kingdom Moments." I liken the Kingdom Moments devotional to little seeds, each day sufficient unto itself.

Each of these seeds represent moments of encounter with the Father in His Kingdom. Each of these seeds when deeply planted in our hearts will sprout Kingdom principles that become opportunities for God encounters. For those who embrace this devotional study in partnership with the Holy Spirit, I believe Kingdom encounters will blossom. The way in which we see life will be through Heaven's eyes. *Kingdom*

Moments is designed to foster intimacy in your relationship with Jesus Christ, your normal will become supernatural.

Hearing God's voice in the present moment is just the beginning of being face-to-face with God, i.e., in His Presence. In Exodus 33:14-16. Moses pleads for God's help. We read...

> *And He [God] said, "My Presence [paniym] will go with you,*
> *and I will give you rest." Then he [Moses] said to Him,*
> *"If Your Presence does not go with us, do not bring us up from here."*

The Hebrew word for Presence is *paniym* which literally means "before one's face, face-to-face." Moses got into the Presence of God, face-to-face, and received a direct, revelation word [*rhema*] from God.

In this devotional, daily workbook, you will have the opportunity to encounter God's written word each day as you seek His face, listen for His still small voice, and humbly receive His specific rhema word for your life. The only time you can truly hear God's present word for you is in His Presence. You are invited by Christ to come unto Him and you, like Moses, will discover peace, rest, and the power to hear and obey His rhema word for you.

Remember that the living, risen Christ has promised not to leave you as an orphan but rather to be your Bread of Life, your Living Water, your Light in darkness, and your Good Shepherd guiding you with His Voice.

I invite you to take this daily journey of **Kingdom Moments** with Christ and experience His abiding and indwelling Presence. Daily discover His amazing promise...

> *No longer do I call you servants,*
> *for a servant does not know what his master is doing;*
> *but I have called you friends,*
> *for all things that I heard from My Father*
> *I have made known to you. (John 15:15)*

"Complacency is a deadly foe of all spiritual growth.
Acute desire must be present or there will be no manifestation
of Christ to His people."
— A.W. Tozer[1]

Today's Rhema Word – Week 1, Day 1

ENCOUNTERING JESUS

But they constrained Him, saying, "Abide with us, f
or it is toward evening, and the day is far spent."
And He went in to stay with them.
(Luke 24:29 NKJV)

This life-changing moment came into the lives of the disciples when Jesus wanted to **encounter** them. In that moment, the two disciples had a longing in their hearts that had gone unmet. They talked about how things once were, and they thought there could never be another time in their lives where they would encounter God in a man.

As they walked with the man Jesus, they persuasively encouraged Him to stay with them a little while longer. To "constrain" means to forcibly take hold of Him, seek His face, and inquire of His guidance, power, direction, and commands for us right now!

Jesus wishes to be *constrained*. He waits for us to take hold of Him. Not for what He can do, but for who He wants to be for us. Their hearts were set ablaze by His Presence. Their hearts burned with the fire of His Spirit.

Don't miss an opportunity to **encounter** Him. Each day, encountering Jesus compels us to Learn, Live, and Love. So, just do it…

Learn from Jesus

"To constrain *means to forcefully compel.*" Constraining Jesus to stay with you and speak to you right now, what would you ask of Him?

_____

_____

Check the distractions that keep you from constraining Jesus to stay with you (✓ all that apply).

Work___ Too Busy___ Guilt___ Shame___ Social Media___ Addiction___
Other People___ TV___ Sports___ Partying___ Internet___

Live for Jesus

When you hear the lyrics from a famous hymn, "Living for Jesus a life that is true; striving to please Him in all that I do…," what do you hear Jesus telling you to do or not to do right now to please Him?

Fill in the name on each line and then circle the three most important *rhema* words you hear:

Forgive __(name)__ Serve __(name)__ Mentor __(name)__
Pray for __(name)__ Lead __(name)__ Follow __(name)__

Love through Jesus

Write a prayer focused on loving others as yourself:

_____

_____

Today's Rhema Word – Week 1, Day 2

MOVE TOWARD YOUR MIRACLE

"But that you may know that the Son of Man has power on earth
to forgive sins"—He said to the man who was paralyzed,
"I say to you, arise, take up your bed, and go to your house."
Immediately he rose up before them, took up what he had been
lying on, and departed to his own house, glorifying God.
And they were all amazed, and they glorified God and were
filled with fear, saying, "We have seen strange things today!"
(Luke 5:24-26 NKJV)

Often a miracle is activated by our movement. First, the man's friends moved toward Jesus. When they couldn't get their friend in the front door, they found an opening in the roof of the house and lowered him down. They believed he would be healed. When Jesus saw the situation, He demonstrated His power without praying for his healing. He simply told the man to **rise**, **take up** his bed, and **walk**. The paralyzed man had to **decide to respond** to Jesus by **moving first** before he could experience the miracle. **His movement activated the miracle.** As he attempted to stand, life returned to his limbs, and he could walk.

Perhaps you've prayed and haven't seen anything yet. An action might be required of you first. Get up and go toward the miracle you're seeking and watch God respond to your faith.

Learn from Jesus

What did this story reveal about accessing the power needed to activate a miracle?

First, the man's friends _____.
Then, Jesus _____.
Immediately, the man _____.

Describe the miracle you are believing for:

_____
_____

What are the steps you need to take to be prepared for your miracle?

_____
_____

Live in Jesus

Look up "miracle" in your Bible concordance and read the New Testament account of the miracles Jesus did. Summarize what the person who received the miracle was required to do. (i.e. John 4:43-54)

_____
_____

Love through Jesus

This paralyzed man had friends who showed their love through their actions. The man's friends moved toward Jesus and found a way to help their friend even when it seemed impossible.

Think of a friend who needs you to show the love of Jesus through your actions. Describe how you are going to accomplish this:

_____
_____

Today's Rhema Word – Week 1, Day 3

SIGNS OF LIFE

So then neither he who plants is anything, nor he who waters,
but God who gives the increase. (1 Corinthians 3:7 NKJV)

I love the springtime. Spring is always marked by the singing of birds and the blossoming of trees. After a winter of silence and barrenness, it is always good to see and hear these signs of life. It reminds us we are alive and should be exhibiting signs of life in our actions every day.

When we allow God to do His work in our lives, when we yield to the Holy Spirit, allowing Him to change us, we will see signs of life and growth within ourselves, and so will others. God is about increase and growth. No matter how hard we try, it's only God who gives increase or spiritual growth. This growth will be reflected in our lives through our character and the fruit of the Spirit shining through our everyday activities and interactions with others.

The cool thing is when you begin to see spiritual growth in the lives of those you lead and influence. Not only is God demonstrating signs of life in you, but He also begins to touch the lives of all those around you. Watching the fruit of life spring up in the ones closest to you is a beautiful thing.

Learn from Jesus

God is about increase. He's about growth. Look around you.
Where do you see signs of life in the natural?

_____

_____

Do you see signs of new life and growth yourself?

_____

_____

Research and describe what happens when a pond becomes stagnant.

_____

_____

Live in Jesus

When we allow God to do His work in our lives and yield to the Holy Spirit, allowing Him to change us, we will see signs of life.

Read Galatians 5:22-23. Describe the Fruit of the Spirit you see growing in your life.

_____

_____

_____

_____

Love through Jesus

What fruit have you seen spring up in those around you as you invest in their lives?

_____

_____

Today's Rhema Word – Week 1, Day 4

REMOVE THE BARRIERS

*"And so my judgment is that we should not make it difficult
for the Gentiles who are turning to God."*
(Acts 15:18 NKJV)

Removing any barriers which might hamper someone who wants to be part of Christ's family is one of North Point Community Church's pastor Andy Stanley's favorite sayings. Andy decided to create a non-religious environment so many non-believing, seeking individuals would be open to attending a weekend service. He discovered it's not just about a church service; it's about an attitude inviting to those outside the body of Christ.

I'm sharing Jesus with two of my neighbors who don't understand religious language or practices, but our conversations show they both are searching for something more. As I've taken the time to get to know them, they are open to talking with me about their lives and struggles. They've been willing to listen to the challenges I have encountered, and the solutions Jesus offered me. Neither has accepted Jesus, but they've heard the gospel and have felt the love of the Father through my words and actions.

As I remove any barriers that might hamper them, Jesus will do the rest.

Learn from Jesus

Circle the ways we may make it difficult for non-believers around us to want to turn to God.

Religious Language Religious Cliches Judgmentalism Criticism Pious Attitude Aggressiveness Not Listening to Them

Live in Jesus

Because I was willing to listen, my neighbors were open to talking with me about their lives and struggles. Then, they were willing to listen to the challenges I have encountered, and the solutions Jesus offered me.

List the people in your area of influence you need to listen to and encourage as a witness of God's love through your compassion.

_____

_____

_____

How can you assist each person on your list?

Love through Jesus

My neighbors heard the gospel in my life story and have felt the love of the Father through my words and actions.

As God leads you, share your testimony with those in your area of influence.

Begin by writing a brief 3–5-minute testimony.

_____

_____

_____

Today's Rhema Word – Week 1, Day 5

THE MORE EXCELLENT WAY

"...And yet I show you a more excellent way."
(1 Corinthians 12:31b NKJV)

What is the more excellent way Paul is referencing here? He's speaking about a life that gives itself to serving and loving others. The context of Chapter 12 is about spiritual gifts. Paul says in verse 7, "But the manifestation of the Spirit is given to each one **for the profit of all**" (NKJV). When God says **all**, He means **all**!

The people in the church at Corinth were skilled in using spiritual gifts and they hungered for more. However, when they started focusing on the gifts, they took their focus off the people the gifts were meant to serve. Then the gifts became about themselves. Paul rebukes them in 1 Corinthians 13:1-3.

Though I speak with the tongues of men and of angels,
*but have not **love**, I have become sounding brass or a clanging cymbal.*
And though I have the gift of prophecy, and understand all mysteries
and all knowledge, and though I have all faith, so that I could remove
*mountains, but have not **love**, I am nothing. And though I bestow all*
my goods to feed the poor, and though I give my body [a]to be burned,
*but have not **love**, it profits me nothing.*
(NKJV emphasis added)

Learn from Jesus

Jesus is all about **love.** His gifts are all about **love.** Everything He does can be traced back to His nature of **love.** The more excellent way Paul is talking about is then explained in Chapter 13:4-7. Fill in the blanks.

Love suffers long *and* is kind; love does not _____; love does not parade itself, is not _____; does not behave _____, does not seek its _____, is not _____, thinks no _____; does not rejoice in _____, but rejoices in the _____, _____ all things, _____ all things, _____ all things, all things. (NKJV)

Live in Jesus

Define the more excellent way Paul is referencing in 1 Corinthians 12:31.

_____

_____

Love through Jesus

The more we love, the more powerful Jesus will manifest Himself through the gifts. Look up and define the love Jesus desires for us to exhibit.

Matthew 7:12

_____

_____

Matthew 5:44

_____

_____

Week 1, Day 6

HEARING & OBEYING GOD'S VOICE

REFLECTION QUESTIONS FOR YOU TO ANSWER THIS WEEK...

1. How is your life an example of "Living for Jesus a life that is true; striving to please Him in all that I do..."?

_____

_____

_____

2. What miracle did you move toward this week, and how did God respond to your faith?

_____

_____

_____

3. How did the Holy Spirit change and grow you this week as you yielded to His work in your life, and how did others respond?

_____

_____

_____

4. Describe how God used you to share your testimony with someone in your area of influence this week:

_____

_____

_____

"God did not direct His call to Isaiah—Isaiah overheard God saying, ". . . who will go for Us?" The call of God is not just for a select few but for everyone. Whether I hear God's call or not depends on the condition of my ears, and exactly what I hear depends upon my spiritual attitude."
— Oswald Chambers, *My Utmost for His Highest*[2]

Today's Rhema Word – Week 2, Day 1

THE CALL OF GOD

The confidence of my calling enables me to overcome every difficulty without shame, for I have an intimate revelation of this God. And my faith in him convinces me that he is more than able to keep all that I've placed in his hands safe and secure until the fullness of his appearing.
(2 Timothy 1:12 TPT)

There is a trust and confidence we must have in the call God has placed on our lives. Another word for call is assignment. Our place in His story is secure; it's certain; it will happen. That call is not only what we will **do for Him**, but it's who we are **in Him**. It doesn't leave anything out.

However, what happens when life gets difficult? What happens when our present circumstances don't quite look like what He's promised?

Simple, we defer back to who He said we are. In His Word, He identifies Himself as "I AM." That means He is the one who has always existed. No one or anything before Him or after Him. He stands at both the beginning of time and the eternal end. That means we are everything God says we are. We can do everything He says we can do, and nothing can stop us.

When difficulties come our way, let's remind ourselves of the Great I AM in Whom we live, move, and have our being.

Learn from Jesus

Read John 17:20-22. Fill in the blanks.

Jesus Prays for All Believers

"I do not pray for these alone, but also for those who [will believe in Me through their word; that they _____ may be _____, as You, Father, *are* in Me, and I in You; that they also may be _____ _____ Us, that the world may believe that You sent Me. And the glory which You gave Me I have given them, that they may be _____ just as We are _____.

Live for Jesus

In John 14:12, what did Jesus tell us as His disciples we would be able to do to fulfill our call if we believe in Him?

_____

_____

Love through Jesus

Look up your favorite miracles of Jesus and describe how He showed His love.

_____

_____

STRENGTHEN THE FAITH OF OTHERS

"But I have prayed for you, Peter, that you would stay faithful
to me no matter what comes. Remember this: after you have
turned back to me and have been restored, make it your
life mission to strengthen the faith of your brothers."
(Luke 22:12 TPT)

P eter owed Jesus His life. Even though he turned his back on Jesus, Jesus never turned His back on him. In fact, Jesus continued to pursue Peter until he was fully restored. He only asked for one thing of Peter, go and strengthen the faith of your brothers.

Every believer should have someone they are strengthening, encouraging, supporting, and mentoring.

You don't have to wait until you are a "super" Christian.

You don't have to wait for a full-time job in ministry.

You should look around your sphere of influence and ask the Father who you can begin strengthening in their faith. Make that a priority. Use the gifts you have to strengthen the faith of those He puts in front of you.

Learn from Jesus

Read Matthew 10:1, 9-10. Describe what Jesus used to strengthen the faith of His disciples:

_____

_____

Live for Jesus

Every believer should have someone they are strengthening, encouraging, supporting, and mentoring. One way is to share your testimony.

Describe an experience that helped you strengthen your own faith.

_____

_____

Love through Jesus

What gifts has God given you that you might be able to use to strengthen the faith of others?

_____

_____

Pray and ask the Father how you can use those gifts to strengthen someone in your sphere of influence this week.

_____

_____

POINT TO JESUS

As Peter was coming in, Cornelius met him and fell down
at his feet and worshiped him. But Peter lifted him up, saying,
"Stand up; I myself am also a man."
(Acts 10:25-26 NKJV)

The reaction Cornelius had to Peter's arrival was that of one who felt he was in the presence of a messenger of God. Peter's statement, "I'm a human being like you," was profound. This act of worship could have caused Peter to become arrogant or prideful. After all, a Roman officer was bowing before him. Instead, Peter pointed Cornelius to Christ. We, too, should remember our own humanity whenever we are flattered or honored and use the opportunity to give glory to God. I believe these are the moments that God tests our hearts to see if we can handle more Kingdom responsibility.

We can never let people build us up or puff us up to be something we are not. No matter how talented we may be, everything we have and all we are comes from our Father in Heaven.

We must respond with a simple *thank you* and do everything in our power to make sure people see Jesus in us. Our desire is that others are inspired to pursue Him the same way we are pursuing Him.

A.W. Tozer wrote, "I want the presence of God Himself, or I don't want anything at all to do with religion... I want all that God has or I don't want any."[34]

Learn from Jesus

Read Philippians 2:5-8. The Amplified Translation says, "Have this same attitude in yourselves which was in Christ Jesus [look to Him as your example…]."

Circle all the words that describe the example Jesus:

humble	passive	meek	unforgiving	obedient
impatient	pious	tolerant	compassionate	kind

Live for Jesus

What did the Apostle Paul say in 1 Corinthians 11:1?

_____

_____

Love through Jesus

God tests our hearts to see how we handle applause, recognition, and being honored. Write out three such tests and honestly grade yourself.

Test 1: A-----B-----C-----D-----E----F
Test 2: A-----B-----C-----D-----E----F
Test 3: A-----B-----C-----D-----E----F

What have you discovered about yourself?
How do you think others would have graded you?

Today's Rhema Word – Week 2, Day 4

WHY DID YOU DOUBT?

And immediately Jesus stretched out His hand and caught him,
*and said to him, "O you of little faith, **why did you doubt?***"
(Matthew 14:31 NKJV emphasis added)

When Jesus got the news His beloved cousin John the Baptist had been beheaded, He went away by Himself to be with the Father. Then, He does the miracle of multiplying the loaves and fishes to feed over 10,000 people. Once He finished, the scripture says He sent the disciples away in a boat, and again He went to be with the Father. Later, the disciples saw Jesus walking on the water. Peter asked Him to call him out of the boat and Peter walked on the water. However, not long into the walk, Peter began looking at the storm and high waves and started to sink. Jesus immediately extended His hand to save Peter and get him back into the boat. When Peter took his eyes off Jesus, he sank.

Taking your eyes off Jesus causes mistakes, failures, and disappointments. However, Jesus doesn't condemn us. Once He sees we are sinking, He wastes no time and extends a hand to save us. He reminds us to use our faith to do the things He is calling us into.

The more we exercise our faith muscle,
the greater the miracles we will experience.

Learn from Jesus

Have you ever worked out or bought muscle-building equipment? List the steps they gave you to be successful and reach your goal:

Step 1:
Step 2:
Step 3:

Live for Jesus

Using the weight-lifting analogy, what three steps did Jesus emulate to show us how to build our faith muscles?

Step 1:
Step 2:
Step 3:

Lift Your Faith with the Words of Jesus

Complete these verses and declare them daily.

Matthew 25:21- Well *done*, good and **faithful** servant;

_____

_____

Luke 16:10 - He who *is* **faithful** in *what is* least is

_____

_____

Today's Rhema Word – Week 2, Day 5

SPIRITUAL GIFTS

As each one has received a gift, minister it to one another,
as good stewards of the manifold grace of God.
(1 Peter 4:10 NKJV)

The gifts from God are given to His sons and daughters to empower us to do His work here on earth. They are a key element to effectively serving Him here on earth. The whole purpose of the gifts is to allow us to do what we are not able to do naturally. As talented as we are, our abilities have limitations. In order to partner with the Father, we need to go outside our human capability through supernaturally enabled gifts.

1 - 1 Corinthians 12:1 says, "Now concerning spiritual gifts, brethren, I do not want you to be ignorant" (NKJV).

2 - 1 Corinthians 12:31a says, "But earnestly desire the best gifts..." (NKJV).

3 - 2 Timothy 1:6 says, "Therefore I remind you to stir up the gift of God which is in you through the laying on of my hands" (NKJV).

The more we minister to those in need in the power of the Holy Spirit using these spiritual gifts, the more gifts our Father will give us.

Learn from Jesus

In John 12:49, Jesus said, "For I have not spoken on My own *authority*; but the Father who sent Me gave Me a command, what I should say and what I should speak."

What lesson was Jesus teaching us in this verse about using spiritual gifts, and why is this so important to understand?

_____

_____

Live for Jesus

Read and list the warnings in 1 Corinthians Chapter 14 about misusing spiritual gifts.

_____

_____

Love through Jesus

That is why I would remind you to stir up (rekindle the embers of, fan the flame of, and keep burning) the [gracious] gift of God, [the inner fire] that is in you. (2 Timothy 1:6 AMPC)

Journal how the Holy Spirit uses you to supernaturally help others.

_____

_____

_____

Week 2, Day 6

HEARING & OBEYING GOD'S VOICE

REFLECTION QUESTIONS FOR YOU TO ANSWER THIS WEEK...

1. When difficulties came your way this week, how did you remind yourself of all God has placed within you to strengthen your faith?

_____

_____

_____

2. How did the way you handled personal recognition give glory to Jesus and inspire others to pursue Him?

_____

_____

_____

3. How has 1 Peter 4:10 become a reality in your life?

As each one has received a gift, minister it to one another, as good stewards of the manifold grace of God. (NKJV)

_____

_____

_____

"True faith rests upon the character of God and asks no further proof than the moral perfections of the One who cannot lie. When all is said and done, the life of faith is nothing if not an unending struggle of the spirit with every available weapon against the flesh."[5]
—A.W. Tozer

"Active faith gives thanks for a promise
even though it is not yet performed,
knowing that God's contracts are as good as cash."
— Matthew Henry[6]

Today's Rhema Word – Week 3, Day 1

RELEASE TRUTH

Jesus turned to Peter and said, "Get out of my way, you Satan! You are an offense to me, because your thoughts are only filled with man's viewpoints and not with the ways of God." (Matthew 16:23 TPT)

Peter wasn't possessed, but he was speaking from the demonic realm. He wasn't drawing upon the wisdom of Heaven. The things he was speaking to Jesus weren't nasty or hurtful; they just weren't true.

The enemy doesn't always come at us in a vile, grotesque way. He simply weaves and mingles his lies with just enough truth to sound convincing. Since he is the Father of lies and his native language is lies, he has become an expert liar. Praise Jesus, the enemy has been dethroned. He huffs and puffs because that's all the power he has. Satan tempts us with our own fleshly thoughts or worldly viewpoints contrary to the ways of God.

God's truth and ways bring us freedom.

When we release Truth, we dismantle the enemy's strategies, and we invite the Holy Spirit into our circumstances.

Learn from Jesus

Read and write out what Jesus said in John 8:32.

_____

_____

Jesus confronted the enemy behind Peter with _____.
Where can you find this powerful weapon? _____.

Live for Jesus

Read John 3:21. "But he who _____ the truth comes to the light, that his deeds may be clearly seen, that they have been done in _____."

Explain how you are going to prepare to accomplish this:

_____

_____

Love through Jesus

Let's be a people of truth and be known for His presence in our lives as we stand against Satan's lies.

Describe a lie Satan has tried to deceive you with and the truth you need to defeat him:

_____

_____

Today's Rhema Word – Week 3, Day 2

STAY ON THE WALL

I have posted watchmen on your walls, O Jerusalem; they will never be silent day or night. You who call on the LORD, give yourselves no rest.
(Isaiah 62:6 NIV)

I saiah's zeal for his people and his desire to see the work of salvation completed caused him to pray without resting, hoping Israel would be saved.

Typically, there would be a night guard on the wall keeping an eye out. Their job was not only securing the people's safety but constant intercession. Isaiah didn't want to leave such an important job to just anyone, so he took it himself.

Be encouraged, imitate the passion of Isaiah, and stay in a place of intercession for the Kingdom of Heaven to be made manifest in your circumstances.

Have you come down off of your wall?
Has the onslaught of the enemy made you weary?

We choose to hope in the salvation of King Jesus over our lives and the people we love. He certainly will do His part, but we must do ours.

Stay on that wall.

Learn from Jesus

Personalize the prayer Jesus taught His disciples. "[My] Father in heaven, hallowed be Your name, Your kingdom come, Your will be done, on earth [in my life and the lives of my loved ones] as it is in heaven. Give [me and my loved ones] our daily bread. Forgive [me for my sins], as [I] also have forgiven [my enemies]. [Help me not to fall off the wall due to the world's temptations or from the enemy's attacks].[7]

Live for Jesus

We should have Isaiah's zeal to see God's will be done in the lives of others. It is good to keep praying persistently for others. This is called intercession.

List those God is calling you to intercede for:

_____

_____

Love through Jesus

Get back up on your wall and consistently intercede.

Refuse to let the onslaught of the enemy make you weary. Stand your ground, stay on the wall!

Today's Rhema Word – Week 3, Day 3

KNOWING GOD'S NATURE

He made known His ways to Moses,
His acts to the children of Israel.
(Psalm 103:7 NKJV)

Which would you prefer: knowing God's ways—which means knowing His character—or observing God's miracles? At first pass, it seems like observing the miracles of God wins hands down. Who wouldn't want to see a huge body of water supernaturally divided in half? Any miracle in the scriptures is awe-inspiring! However, contrast the opportunity to see amazing signs, miracles, and wonders with the privilege of *knowing God's very nature.* Perhaps it doesn't seem as exciting, but God revealed to Moses the power behind the miracles.

To know God's nature is to know the secret behind the success. It's to have the keys to whatever you want in this life.

As sons and daughters, we have access to Father God's nature. He wants us to know His heart and His ways. He's wide open. Spend time getting to know our Father's heart and His ways.

Learn from Jesus

Do you want to know God's nature? _____

Jesus is the epitome of our Heavenly Father. Record what you learn from Jesus about God's nature:

John 6:25-46

Luke 15:11-32

Live for Jesus

Do you want to be a living demonstration of the awesome things God can do? _____Start here:

Very truly I tell you, whoever believes in me _____ ___ the _____ I have been doing, and they will do even _____ _____ than these, because I am going to the Father. And I will do whatever you _____ in my name, so that the Father may be glorified in the Son. (John 14:12-13 NIV)

Love through Jesus (go and do)

Do you want to go behind the scenes and be part of "making the movie," not just watching it?

How are you going to implement Mark 16:15-18?

_____

_____

Today's Rhema Word – Week 3, Day 4

LET'S MOVE OUT!

*Now faith is the substance of things hoped for, t
he evidence of things not seen.*
(Hebrews 11:1 NKJV)

L et's explore how faith works. The things God has for His sons and
daughters are unseen. They begin in the spiritual realm. God puts
in our spirit the things He wants to be ours. What we experience is a
deep certainty within that whatever it is, is coming to us. What we are
experiencing is the substance, the evidence, the proof that what God
has for us is certainly on its way. It's tangible. It's real and undeniable
inside of us. When it comes to us, no one can tell us it's not real. That's
how faith works.

Though we don't see what's coming, the evidence that it's enroute
is inside. Faith deposits inside of us a demand to move out in action.
When we move out in action, God meets us with the promise, and what
was once unseen materializes and becomes real and is seen by all. Our
job is to learn how to move out in action on the deposits of faith God
puts in us.

Let's move out.

Learn from Jesus

Describe the important lesson about faith Jesus showed us in John 11:38-44.

_____

_____

Live for Jesus

Let's do a personal assessment. How would you describe your level of faith?

weak…. somewhat strong…. very strong

Love through Jesus (go and do)

Our job is to learn how to move out in action on the deposits of faith God puts in us. Let's move out.

Read what Jesus said in Luke 7:9.

Declare:

> ➤ I will move out in faith so Jesus will declare this over me!

Read Matthew 9:21-22.
Declare:

> ➤ I will take action so I will receive God's promises today!

Today's Rhema Word – Week 3, Day 5

MAKING A DIFFERENCE

True spirituality that is pure
in the eyes of our Father God
is to make a difference in the lives of the orphans,
and widows in their troubles,
and to refuse to be corrupted by the world's values.
(James 1:27 TPT)

F aith is active, alive and targets the marginalized, the vulnerable, the least, the lost, and the unlovely. As we allow faith to have its outward expression, it leads us to those in need, especially the vulnerable. Something beautiful happens as we serve those who have no voice.

Our values and ways of living begin to line up with the values and way of life of Jesus. The things that are important to the world are less important to us. The desires we have in this world start to look like the desires in Daddy's heart. We literally are shielded from being corrupted by the world's values.

When we stop looking at ourselves and look at the hurting world around us, including family, we become overwhelmed with compassion and love. We desperately seek answers and wisdom from Papa God, and He responds in and through His beloved—us.

Learn from Jesus

What have you done that constitutes making a difference in the lives of the orphans, widows, and vulnerable in the eyes of Father God?

Feeding the hungry   Clothing for homeless
Protecting the vulnerable   Praying for the sick

Live for Jesus

Read these scriptures and record what Jesus did in each situation.
Matthew 14:15-21
Matthew 19:14
Luke 8:21
John 8:1-11

Love through Jesus (go and do)

When Jesus walked the earth, He asked Father God who needed His help. Make that your prayer today and every day as well.

What need around you is the Holy Spirit revealing? How are you going to respond? _____
_____

Week 3, Day 6

HEARING & OBEYING GOD'S VOICE

REFLECTION QUESTIONS FOR YOU TO ANSWER THIS WEEK...

1. How did faith and truth work together in your life this week to ful-fill God's will on the earth through you, His beloved?

    _____

    _____

    _____

2. How did you display "Now faith" in your life this week?

    _____

    _____

    _____

3. How did you move out in faith and make a difference in others' lives this week?

    _____

    _____

    _____

"Do all the good you can,
By all the means you can,
In all the ways you can,
In all the places you can,
At all the times you can,
To all the people you can,
As long as ever you can."

— John Wesley[8]

GOD'S ARMY IS WITH YOU

"Yet I have reserved seven thousand in Israel,
all whose knees have not bowed to Baal,
and every mouth that has not kissed him."
(1 Kings 19:18 NKJV)

In one of the most powerful stories in the Bible, Elijah has another power encounter with the Living God. He's witnessed a mass slaughter by Jezebel of hundreds of God's prophets. Though there were one hundred hidden in mountain caves, Elijah felt alone. He felt it was over for him. Though he'd seen God bring down fire from heaven and so many other signs, miracles, and wonders, he felt he was doomed.

Read 1 Kings 19:11-12.

Stay connected to God's voice. Forget about the delivery vehicle. Listen up and wait to hear what He says next. Once Elijah heard God's voice, it was revealed that 7000 prophets and faithful followers were aligned and ready to continue walking with God. Elijah immediately realized he wasn't really alone. It was deception at its finest. Don't believe it when the enemy comes and tells you you're alone or it's over. It's a lie!

Learn from Jesus

Jesus has surrounded you with thousands, not just in the spirit but also in the natural. He'll send in reinforcements just when it's most needed.

- ➢ **Stay faithful.**
- ➢ **Stay full of the Holy Spirit.**
- ➢ **Be courageous.**

Live for Jesus

Read and memorize 1 John 4:4.
Declare it daily!

Love through Jesus (go and do)

Don't believe it when the enemy comes and tells you you're alone or you can't do it. It's a lie! Are you being attacked by the enemy as you prepare to move out and do what God is telling you to do?

Read Matthew 28:18. It gives you the authority, now go and do what Jesus said to do in Matthew 28:19-20.

Today's Rhema Word – Week 4, Day 2

SPEAK A WORD IN SEASON

"The Lord GOD has given Me the tongue of the learned, that I should know how to speak a word in season to him who is weary. He awakens Me morning by morning; He awakens My ear to hear as the learned."
(Isaiah 50:4 NKJV)

This is the life we've been called to live. We are fathered by the God of all creation. This relationship is real, it's personal, and it's relevant for now. God has things to say to His sons and daughters and things we are to accomplish for Him.

Make no mistake about it, He has an agenda.

Our words and actions will only have the power that comes from Heaven if we get them from the Lord. It requires us to be ever so close to Him. He wants to teach us and show us His way of life and love. Our connection with the Father should be seamless, an unbroken connection. We know this life we've been called to works. This is what we are all about.

We need to learn how to use what Jesus has given us to help those who are weary!

Learn from Jesus

How did Jesus describe you in Matthew 5:14?

_____

_____

What is the source of your power?

_____

_____

What are you supposed to do with what He's given you?

_____

_____

Live for Jesus

Who are the ones who should be the first to receive from this power Jesus has given you?

_____

_____

Love through Jesus (go and do)

What are you supposed to go and do with this power Jesus has filled you with?

_____

_____

_____

Don't Miss the Move of God

The sick man answered Him, "Sir, I have no man to put me into the pool when the water is stirred up; but while I am coming, another steps down before me." Jesus said to him, "Rise, take up your bed and walk."
(John 5:7-8 NKJV)

The story goes that an angel would come down and stir the water in the pool of Bethesda and those who jumped in the water quickly would be healed. Well, every time that would happen, the lame man would miss it.

How many moves of God have we missed?

I'm not talking about earth-shaking moments. I'm referring to times when God has moved left, and we have veered right. Or God says straight ahead and we're standing still. The paralyzed man continued to miss the moves of God for 38 years. *Why?*

The two interesting things Jesus told him to do were to **get up** and **bring his mat with him**. *Why?*

Be sensitive to the moves of God around you, be ready to obey and carry your earthly belongings with you so you won't miss out. Then, no turning back!

Learn from Jesus

Think about what Jesus **did** and **did not do** for the lame man. Circle how you would describe yourself in each one:

An enabler or an equipper?

An instructor or a lecturer?

A doer or an observer?

Live for Jesus

How did Jesus teach His disciples to be fishers of men?

_____

_____

Love through Jesus (go and do)

As a disciple of Jesus, describe how He really desires for you to help others around you. Remember, you cannot be around them 24 hours a day. For example, what is the best way to teach your child proper respect for others even when you are not with them?

_____

_____

_____

_____

Today's Rhema Word – Week 4, Day 4

FEAR AND FAITH DON'T MIX

Now they came to Jericho. As He went out of Jericho with His disciples and a great multitude, blind Bartimaeus, the son of Timaeus, sat by the road begging. And when he heard that it was Jesus of Nazareth, he began to cry out and say, "Jesus, Son of David, have mercy on me!"
(Mark 10:46-47 NKJV)

J esus loves invitations. There are some things He will only do if you are not afraid to invite Him.

What is it that you need Jesus to do for you today?

Have you invited Him to come near you?

Jesus responds to our invitations of need. However, before we ever open our mouths, we posture our hearts in faith believing He is who He said He is, and He can do what He said He can do.

This blind man was desperate. In his mind, he felt he had nothing to lose and everything to gain. He didn't care that it was inappropriate in his day to call out to such an important person from the roadside. He didn't mind being ridiculed or mocked. Fear of man was gone. I believe all these things were in place before he ever opened his mouth.

Learn from Jesus

Where in your mind and heart are you stuck?

What stops you from extending the invitation to Jesus?

> *Then Jesus said to him, "Go your way; your faith has made you well." And immediately he received his sight and followed Jesus on the road.* (Mark 10:52)

Jesus said, "Your faith has made you well."
Read these verses and use them to write a definition of faith according to God's Word.

Romans 10:17 says faith is: _____
Hebrews 11:1 says faith is: _____
Faith is _____

Live for Jesus

Our lives reflect whether we live by faith or fear. Describe what it means to live by faith, not by fear.

See Matthew 21:21, 2 Corinthians 5:7, Hebrews 13:6.

_____

_____

Love through Jesus (go and do)

Ask God to show you how to use your faith to pray for and help others as you begin each day.

Today's Rhema Word – Week 4, Day 5

SUPERCHARGE YOUR LIFE

Having a form of godliness but denying its power...
(2 Timothy 3:5 NKJV)

To be a follower of Jesus, as understood in the Gospels and the book of Acts, is to have a life completely powered by the Holy Spirit. This spiritually powered life produces a visible lifestyle that bears biblical fruit.

Without the power, a person is left to just going through the motions. That's the definition of being religious. The motions of Christianity without the power of Christ will produce no lasting fruit. Jesus calls us to bear fruit that will remain. Don't fall into the trap of motions, saying all the right things, doing what appears to be right, but lacking the power of the Holy Spirit.

Through fellowship with the Holy Spirit, you will always find your life powered and divinely supercharged. That's the kind of life we want to live. Those are the people we want to do life with.

Supercharge your life in the Holy Spirit.

But you shall receive power (ability, efficiency, and might) when the Holy Spirit has come upon you, and you shall be My witnesses in Jerusalem and all Judea and Samaria and to the ends (the very bounds) of the earth. (Acts 1:8 AMPC)

Complete each of the following verses.

Learn from Jesus

"I am the vine; you *are* the branches. He who _____ in Me, and I in him, bears much _____; for _____Me you can do _____." (John 15:5 NKJV)

"If you abide in Me, and My words abide in you, you will ask what you desire, and it shall be done for you. By this My Father is glorified, that you _____ much _____; so, you will be My _____." (John 15:7-8 NKJV)

Live for Jesus

"Abide in Me, and I in you. As the branch _____ bear fruit of itself, unless it _____ in the vine, neither can you, _____ you abide in Me." (John 15:4 NKJV)

Love through Jesus (go and do)

"You did not choose Me, but I chose you and appointed you that you should ____ and bear fruit, and *that* your _____ should _____, that whatever you ask the Father in My name He may give you." (John 15:16 NKJV)

Week 4, Day 6

HEARING & OBEYING GOD'S VOICE

REFLECTION QUESTIONS FOR YOU TO ANSWER THIS WEEK...

D on't fall into the trap of going through the motions, saying all the right things, doing what appears to be right, but lacking the power of the Holy Spirit. Through fellowship with the Holy Spirit, you will always find your life powered and divinely supercharged. That's the kind of life we want to live. Those are the people we want to do life with.

1. *Are you more aware of how your actions and words might be lacking the power of the Holy Spirit? Have there been times when you felt like you were just going through the motions? What, if anything, did you discover you needed to change?*

    _____

    _____

    _____

2. *How can you connect with others who are also seeking to live the Holy Spirit supercharged life? How do you think this would improve your life?*

    _____

    _____

    _____

"The Christian leader of the future is called to be completely irrelevant and to stand in this world with nothing to offer but his or her own vulnerable self. That is the way Jesus came to reveal God's love. The great message that we must carry, as ministers of God's Word and followers of Jesus, is that God loves us not because of what we do or accomplish, but because God has created and redeemed us in love and has chosen us to proclaim that love as the true source of all human life."

— Henri J.M. Nouwen,

In the Name of Jesus: Reflections on Christian Leadership[9]

"The test of a preacher is that people don't say
'What a lovely sermon!' but, 'I will do something!'"

— Francis de Sales[10]

Today's Rhema Word – Week 5, Day 1

MOTHERS OF MULTITUDES

Then God said to Abraham, "As for Sarai your wife, you shall not call
her name Sarai, but Sarah shall be her name. And I will bless her
and also give you a son by her; then I will bless her, and she shall be a
mother of nations; kings of peoples shall be from her."
(Genesis 17:15-16 NKJV)

I n Puerto Rico, Madre de Multitudes (mother of multitudes) was a blessing we pronounced over young girls and women whether they had children of their own or not. It was a faith confession saying they were called to be spiritual mothers to thousands.

Sarai means "quarrelsome or contentious," but God Himself changed her name to Sarah meaning mother of nations. Her name declared her destiny. In the Hebrew culture, names have meaning. When the name is spoken, everyone knows the meaning. Anytime anyone said, "Hi, Sarah," it was the same as saying, "Hi, mother of nations." God wanted this confession made over Sarah for the rest of her life.

Speak this faith confession over all the women in your life and those who are active in your church family. Then they will know they are called to be spiritual mothers to many. Read about the spiritual influence of Lydia in Acts 16:14, 49. She became a spiritual mother to many as the Christian church began to grow.

Learn from Father God

In the Hebrew culture, names have meaning. When the name is spoken, everyone knows the meaning. Father God personally named some of His sons and daughters in the Bible.

Abram became _____ which means _____

_____.

Sarai became _____ which means _____

_____.

Jesus or Immanuel means _____.

Live for Jesus

Why are the meanings of our names so important?

_____

When people hear your name, what do they think of?

_____

What does calling yourself a Christian tell others?

_____

Does your life live up to the name Christian? _____
Why or why not? _____

Love through Jesus (go and do)

Read John 13:34-35.
How are you to go and do what a disciple of Jesus is supposed to do?

_____

_____

Today's Rhema Word – Week 5, Day 2

PAUL'S ADVICE FOR MINISTRY

Meditate on these things; give yourself entirely to them,
that your progress may be evident to all.
(1 Timothy 4:15 NKJV)

Attention all young followers and ministers. This is probably some of the best advice you can receive. Paul is writing to his young disciple Timothy. He tells him not to let anyone allow his youthfulness to be a barrier to ministry. Certainly, youth can be a huge barrier to effective ministry if one is not careful.

Take time to read the earlier verses as you complete the interactive section on the next page. Paul gives some sound advice. In verse 15, he pauses in his advice and tells Timothy to meditate on the things that he shared. As one called by God, there will be a lot of choices and decisions you will make in your life that will affect the future direction of your ministry in Christ. However, if you allow God to weigh in, most certainly you will make great decisions and it will be evident to everyone.

Paul wanted to make sure there was no doubt left in the mind of Timothy's community that he was anointed and called by God for the work at hand.

Remember, we are all called to be ministers of the Gospel for our Lord!

Learn from Apostle Paul

Check out Paul's advice in the following verses so you can live and minister for Jesus:

1 Timothy 4:1 says beware of those who abandon _____ and follow _____.

1 Timothy 4:3 says they also forbid people to _____ and abstain from _____.

1 Timothy 4:6 says: _____

Live for Jesus

Commit your life to the things Paul outlines below and your life and ministry will be amazing.

1 Timothy 4:7-8 warns_____

_____

1 Timothy 4:9-11 instructs _____

_____

Love through Jesus (go and do)

1 Timothy 4:12 says, _____

_____

1 Timothy 4:13 says, _____

_____

1 Timothy 4:16 says if you, _____

_____

Today's Rhema Word – Week 5, Day 3

A Portal to God's Power

*But he answered me, "My grace is always more than enough for you,
and my power finds its full expression through your weakness." So I will
celebrate my weaknesses, for when I'm weak I sense more deeply
the mighty power of Christ living in me. So I'm not defeated by my
weakness, but delighted! For when I feel my weakness and endure
mistreatment—when I'm surrounded with troubles on every side and
face persecution because of my love for Christ—I am made yet stronger.
For my weakness becomes a portal to God's power.*
(2 Corinthians 12:9-10 TPT)

This is one of those passages that we've heard quoted often in sermons. It's Paul talking about his weaknesses because he received an important revelation from Father God. Human weakness is the entry point for God's presence and power. I've spent my life covering up my weaknesses, playing them down, and outright avoiding them. However, as my appetite for more of God has grown, this is where the Holy Spirit seems to be leading me. The Passion Translation says our weakness is a portal. If it's how God shows up, then it's worth it. That's why Paul said he celebrates his weaknesses.

**Every time we discover a weakness and
invite God into our weakness,
we see Him in a new and fresh way.
Learn from Apostle Paul**

God told Paul, "My _____ is always more than enough for you, and my _____ finds its ____ expression through **your** _____."

Paul said, "When I'm _____ I sense more deeply the mighty _____ of Christ living ___ _____. So I'm not _____ by my _____, but _____! I will _____ my weaknesses."

Live for Jesus

Living in the Kingdom is about what we can't do without Him. It's about Jesus! It's about making room for Him to be God, to be the savior, healer, and deliverer to a broken world.

Are you ready to take on this challenge?

Will you stop covering up your weaknesses, playing them down, and outright avoiding them?

Love through Jesus (go and do)

Invite God into your weakness, discover Him in a new and fresh way, and then go out and love through Jesus by letting Him be God in each of your challenges today!

Today's Rhema Word – Week 5, Day 4

FILL THE RELATIONAL GAP

*For I know the plans I have for you," declares the LORD, "plans to
prosper you and not to harm you, plans to give you hope and a future.
Then you will call upon me and come and pray to me,
and I will listen to you. You will seek me and find me
when you seek me with all your heart.*
(Jeremiah 29:11-13 NIV)

The Children of Israel were being freed from Babylonian captivity.
Years of slavery had shaped their thoughts about themselves and
their future. We experience slavery when we are in sin, and it shapes
our thoughts about ourselves and our future.

Jesus has freed us from sin and the grave, but even in our freedom,
we carry the mindset of slavery. All we see is what's in front of us. The
idea of having a powerful future often eludes us.

God has plans that look and feel good and are meant to be a blessing
to us and to everyone around us. The closer we get to the Father, the
closer He comes to us, and the more aware we become of our life
and future.

I would go so far as to say if there is uncertainty about your future,
the Father wants you to close the relational gap. *Are you experiencing
that uncertainty?*

Learn from Jesus

It is time to take that **step of faith**.

What slavery mindsets do you need to take out of your backpack in order to close the gap to God?

_____

_____

→You are here →God is here →Your Future is here

Live for Jesus

God has plans that look good and feel good and are meant to be a blessing to you and to everyone around you. He often only shows you the first step.

What has God revealed as your first step?

_____

_____

Take **a step of faith** even if you don't understand it.

Love through Jesus (go and do)

Look to Jesus. Go hard after Him. Become a sponge absorbing everything He puts in front of you. As you pursue the Father, your future will be unveiled right before you.

Don't be afraid to take that step of faith!

Today's Rhema Word – Week 5, Day 5

LEAD WITH THE END IN MIND

And there is no creature hidden from His sight,
but all things are naked and open to the eyes of Him
to whom we must give account.
(Hebrews 4:13 NKJV)

I have had the opportunity to lead mission teams to various places around the world. When the trip is over, the team has an opportunity to fill out a survey to access their experiences—good or bad. When all surveys are complete, we receive a report that lets us know how we did. If we lead poorly, trip participants will most certainly comment. I have created a strategy, knowing that at the conclusion of every trip we will receive an assessment of our leadership. "Lead with the end in mind." That simply means leading the team with those criteria firmly in your mind. Lead knowing you will be evaluated at the end of your mission.

The same is true with our Heavenly Father. We all will have to give an account to Him for how we have lived. Knowing that all we have done and will do will be accounted for, let's live and lead with the end in mind. We don't have to be anxious or paranoid in living for Christ like "Big Brother" is watching us. We just need to live full of the Holy Spirit who has been given to us in order that we might live, lead, and love well.

Live...lead...love with the end in mind.

Learn from Jesus

Jesus left us an example of how to lead with the end in mind. Read these scriptures and record what He is teaching you about leading.

Mark 10:40-45 _____

Luke 6:31 _____

Acts 20:28 _____

John 13:12-17 _____

Live for Jesus

Jesus called Himself the Good Shepherd. He fulfilled everything that was said about Him in Psalm 23. List what a Good Shepherd does as you lead your flock, whether it's family, neighbors, co-workers, or church ministry (paid or volunteer).

_____

_____

_____

_____

_____

Lead like Jesus (go and do)

Read 1 Peter 5:1-4. Jesus led and taught Peter and the other disciples how to go and fulfill their calling to lead others. You have that same calling on your life. Now, go and do it!

Week 5, Day 6

HEARING & OBEYING GOD'S VOICE

REFLECTION QUESTIONS FOR YOU TO ANSWER THIS WEEK...

This week you gleaned a lot of wisdom from the Apostle Paul, Jesus, and God Himself.

1. *As you review what you learned this week, what impacted you the most in your life?*

    _____

    _____

    _____

2. *What has helped you the most as you minister in the Kingdom of God?*

    _____

    _____

    _____

3. *What leadership skills are you going to be able to implement right away as you work toward completing your God mission?*

    _____

    _____

    _____

"There are no 'ifs' in God's world.
And no places that are safer than other places.
The center of His will is our only safety - let us pray that we may
always know it!"

— Corrie Ten Boom[11]

"The will of God is not something you add to your life. It's a course
you choose. You either line yourself up with the Son of God...or you
capitulate to the principle which governs the rest of the world."

— Elisabeth Elliot[12]

RUN THIS RACE WITH PASSION

Therefore, since we are surrounded by such a great cloud of witnesses, let us throw off everything that hinders and the sin that so easily entangles, and let us run with perseverance the race marked out for us.
(Hebrews 12:1 NIV)

Not only do we have access to the resources from Heaven, we also have a whole entourage of people who have gone before us literally cheering us on. Sometimes, I wish it were possible to see or hear all those heroes in scripture and of the revivals we've read about in books. Our personal heroes (in my case, my father, grandfather, and great-grandfather) and so many others who've given their lives for Jesus are shouting things from Heaven like: "This faith is real. You need to know that there is a specific path God has mapped out for you. Don't go over there. Leave that alone. Get to know the Father. Don't grieve or quench the Holy Spirit."

Whether we can see or hear them or not, it's a reality that encourages us to go after the life Jesus has set before us with all we have.

Let's encourage one another to run this race with passion and total obedience.

Learn from the Great Cloud of Witnesses

Think about your favorite hero of faith from the scripture and one personal hero.

Who are they? How are they encouraging you to run your race with passion and obedience?

_____

_____

Live for Jesus

Read Proverbs 13:22.

How is your life encouraging those around you to run their race with passion and obedience?

_____

_____

What is the legacy you are leaving behind for those who are following in your footsteps?

_____

_____

Love through Jesus (go and do)

Pray and ask the Holy Spirit who Jesus is directing you to encourage to run this race with passion and total obedience.

List them and what you need to do to begin to follow God's plan to be this encourager.

_____

_____

Go and do what He is telling you to do starting today!

Today's Rhema Word – Week 6, Day 2

HUNGRY FOR HEAVENLY FOOD

*I open my mouth and inhale the word of God because I crave the
revelation of your commands. Turn your heart to me, Lord,
and show me your grace like you do to every one of your godly lovers.*
(Psalm 119:131-132 TPT)

Looking out of our bedroom window at a beautiful golf course surrounded by pristine wilderness, I see a place that screams God and makes me thankful and hungry for food from the heavenly table. I love the Word and read it with an insatiable appetite, mining for its nuggets, and the priceless jewels of revelation. Hunger precedes revelation. Revelation comes from spending time in God's Word. There is no substitute.

As we spend time in His Word, He turns His heart toward us. As a good Father, He delights in sharing the mysteries of His Kingdom with His children. I no longer read God's Word for information. I read it for transformation and revelation.

I pray and ask the Holy Spirit to guide me into His truth, teach me what He wants me to know, and show me what He wants me to see. I pray for Him to reveal to me who God is and what He wants me to do.

Falling in love with Jesus is falling in love with His Word.

Learn from Jesus

The Word of God is filled with powerful nuggets of truth and revelation.

Does the time you spend mining for these nuggets show Father God you are truly thankful and hungry for food from His heavenly table? _____

_____

Do you read it with an insatiable appetite for His nuggets and the price-less jewels of revelation? _____

What adjustments do you need to make in your time seeking transformation and revelation?

_____

_____

Live for Jesus

Read and complete John 14:26. "But the Comforter, who is the Holy Ghost whom the Father will send in My name, He shall _____ you _____ things and bring _____ things to your remembrance, what-soever I have said unto you" (KJV).

Love through Jesus (go and do)

Pray this prayer, *"Holy Spirit, guide me into all truth, teach me what God wants me to know, and show me what He wants me to see. I pray for You to reveal to me who God is and what He wants me to do."* Amen!

Today's Rhema Word – Week 6, Day 3

THE RIDE OF YOUR LIFE

For it is God who works in you both
to will and to do for His good pleasure.
(Philippians 2:13 NKJV)

It's incredible to know that Father God gets pleasure seeing His plans play out in our lives. It's also important to note that there are two parts to His plan in our life's story. There is the actual plan itself with many details, timelines, destinations, and people involved. Having walked with Jesus for several decades, I get the privilege of looking back and seeing how His plan has been played out in my life. I can see His timeline. In fact, I charted a timeline of significant activities in my journey. I can see the big and small destinations that were around the corner, on the side of the road, at work, and the significant spiritual fathers and brothers I have ministered with, and men I have or am discipling.

The second part is all of Heaven's resources to carry out His plan. Being baptized in the Holy Spirit, speaking in tongues, and learning about and using various supernatural gifts. He showed me my Jesus calling from Ephesians 4:11. The good news is what God does for one He does for all in many different ways. He will continue to do so until we see Him face-to-face.

Hold on family, you are in for the ride of your life.

Learn from Jesus

Have you sought all of Heaven's resources to carry out His plan for your life?

*Have you been baptized in the Holy Spirit and speak in tongues or some other manifestation? (See Acts 1:5, 8)*_____

Have you learned about and used various supernatural gifts? (See Romans 12:4-8) _____

Are you one who has a Jesus calling from Ephesians 4:11?

Live for Jesus

Father God gets pleasure seeing His plans play out in our lives. Create a timeline of your journey with Jesus.

What details, destinations, and people have you already encountered and experienced in your journey so far?

_____

_____

What new details, timelines, destinations, and people has God shown you to use as you move forward with your life journey?

_____

_____

Love through Jesus (go and do)

Prepare for the ride of your life as He has revealed it so far and then go and start your amazing ride!

My Preparation Plans include:

_____

_____

Today's Rhema Word – Week 6, Day 4

LOVE IS LIKE A RIVER

I continue to pray for your love to grow and increase beyond measure,
bringing you into the rich revelation of spiritual insight in all things.
This will enable you to choose the most excellent way of all—becoming
pure and without offense until the unveiling of Christ.
(Philippians 1:9-10 TPT)

P aul hits on something I've been exploring for a while. He connects love and deeper spiritual revelation. In fact, it seems there is no deeper spiritual revelation without love. I believe we all desire deeper spiritual revelation.

Father God wants us to share His heart for people. He wants us to feel the love He feels for them all. When we tie into the Father's love, we tie into His heart, His thoughts about us, others, and our circumstances.

Love is like a river, and He's calling us to follow its flow. Where it leads is what He's doing. I can't say I have it figured out, but I believe I'm on the right track.

I continue to pray for your love to grow and increase beyond measure,
bringing you into the rich revelation of spiritual insight in all things and
to choose the most excellent path of all.

Learn from Heart of God

Write a definition of the heart of God using the following scriptures:

1 John 3:1 says, _____

1 John 4:8 says, _____

1 John 4:16 says, _____

Definition:

_____

_____

Live for Jesus

How have you demonstrated God's heart to others?

Helping   Kindness   Thoughtfulness
Giving   Connecting   Works   Errands
        Time   Talents   Encouragement
Feeding the poor   Praying   Visiting the sick

Love through Jesus (go and do)

How did Jesus display God's heart of love? (See Matthew 14:14, 32; Mark 6:34; John 17:20-21.)

_____

_____

_____

Today go and follow Jesus' examples!

Today's Rhema Word – Week 6, Day 5

ALIGNMENT

*For I have come down from heaven not to do my will
but to do the will of him who sent me.*
(John 6:38 NIV)

The Cambridge Dictionary defines alignment as an arrangement in which two or more things are positioned in a straight line or parallel to each other.[13] God has drawn a line that marks our course on this earth. He's at the beginning and the end of the line. The Holy Spirit is our guide who has been tasked to aid in keeping us aligned with the Father. Our responsibility is to daily make certain we are in alignment with the Father's will.

Often our own desires or the desires of someone else's will are superimposed over our life. In either case, it takes maturity to stay in line with what Father God is doing. When God's will lead us to go to Puerto Rico as missionaries, there were many respected people in our life who thought otherwise. However, we were intimately tied to what the Father was doing, and His will became obvious to all. We went forward with His plan. He even loosened our heartstrings to make it easier to leave our friends and family behind. It was one of the hardest and easiest decisions we have ever made in our lives.

Learn from Jesus

Draw a set of parallel railroad tracks with God at the train station and at the end destination. Add a simple train engine and one passenger car. The Holy Spirit is the engineer, and you are one of the passengers. Draw destination signs along the way.

What will happen if the railroad tracks come out of alignment even by a small amount? _____

What if the other passengers try to talk you into getting off at the wrong stops along the way? _____

Live for Jesus

God's will is real and He desires us to be in perfect alignment with it even if it's difficult.

Wouldn't you rather be in the center of His will than the middle of your own? _____

How can you know and live in God's perfect will? (See Romans 12:2.)
_____
_____

Love through Jesus (go and do)

Jesus knew and followed God's will all His life even as He prayed prior to His crucifixion (see Matthew 26:39.) Make your prayer the same as His prayer.

Week 6, Day 6

HEARING & OBEYING GOD'S VOICE

REFLECTION QUESTIONS FOR YOU TO ANSWER THIS WEEK...

This week you learned how to discover and follow God's heart and His will for your life so you can **run this race with passion and stay in alignment with His perfect will for your life's mission.**

1. *As you considered those who came before you, how did the legacy they left you impact your life's choices?*

   _____

   _____

2. *How have you adjusted your life to reflect God's heart of love to others within your area of influence?*

   _____

   _____

   _____

3. *Have you experienced outside influences that tried to move you out of alignment with God's plan and path for your journey?* _____

   How will you handle these situations in the future?

   _____

   _____

"Praise and worship is not about how talented you are or what a wonderful and beautiful voice you have. It's all about denying yourself, let God to be God in your life and praise Him with all your heart and soul."

— Euginia Herlihy[14]

Today's Rhema Word – Week 7, Day 1

DROP ANCHOR

For I am the LORD, I do not change...
(Malachi 3:6a NKJV)

God says, "I DO NOT change." In this generation, things change overnight. Often the shifts are so strong in our society, we are swept away by the collective influence. Our minds, our emotions, and our feelings are always changing depending on the circumstances.

Change isn't bad, but there must be a constant. There must be a true north. There must be a way to calibrate to determine where we are in light of an ever-changing world. No matter what is happening in our world, God remains a constant. We can count on Him. If everyone abandons us, He's there. If truth changes, His Truth is absolute. He's like an anchor. When we drop anchor in our soul, no matter what happens, it will be impossible for us to get off course. The anchor is Jesus, the living Word spoken of in John.

Know His Word. Know Him intimately.

Make sure your anchor is set. When the winds of life blow and the waves of circumstance beat against your life, you can look to Jesus and be assured He's got you!

Learn from Jesus

Read John 1-2. The anchor is Jesus, the living Word.

Read Luke 6:46-49.

Describe the wise builder.

_____

_____

Describe the foolish builder.

_____

_____

Live for Jesus

Read Hebrews 6:17-20.

What are the two unchangeable things God declared in these verses?

_____

_____

Jesus Christ is our anchor. Like an anchor holding a ship safely in position, our faith in Christ guarantees our safety. It holds us safely in our position in Christ.

Love through Jesus (go and do)

Remember, your life is a living testimony of how you handle the winds of change and the waves of circumstance that beat against your life.

Today's Rhema Word – Week 7, Day 2

THE JOY OF THE LORD

He will yet fill your mouth with laughing,
and your lips with rejoicing.
(Job 8:21 NKJV)

Nehemiah said that the joy of the Lord is our strength (8:10). I'm totally wide open to knowing and experiencing the Lord in different ways that I feel still line up with scripture. We were at a conference being ministered to where the burdens we had been experiencing were lifted. As we got to the place where we were seated, we looked at each other and immediately began to laugh. It was like something springing up from the inside. We didn't laugh very long, though we both knew it was something special. I believe there are moments, whether we are in a ministry environment or in our home when we become overcome with laughter.

I believe laughter is at times tied to joy. I will confess I still don't fully understand why Nehemiah says that the joy of the Lord is our strength. Joy must be like the oxygen in the atmosphere of Heaven. God is truly good!

Let the joy of our Lord overwhelm your soul.

Learn from David in Psalms

Write out and memorize these psalms:

Psalm 32:7 _____

_____

Psalm 32:11 _____

_____

Psalm 4:6-7 _____

_____

Live for Jesus

Nehemiah 8:10 says: _____

How do you build strength in your physical body? _____

_____

How often do you do this? _____

How do you build strength in your spiritual body? _____

_____

How often should you do this? _____

Love through Jesus (go and do)

Allow yourself to express your joy in the Lord whatever you are doing and wherever you are going throughout your day. Wear a smile on your face, walk with a bounce in your step, and greet others with a joyful countenance. You will be amazed at the responses you encounter from others. You will encourage them to smile and uplift them in their day.

Today's Rhema Word – Week 7, Day 3

THE SPIRIT OF HUMILITY

Likewise you younger people, submit yourselves to your elders.
Yes, all of you be submissive to one another, and be clothed with
humility, for God resists the proud, but gives grace to the humble.
Therefore humble yourselves under the mighty hand of God,
that He may exalt you in due time.
(1 Peter 5:5-7 NKJV)

I was listening to a panel of godly elder men in ministry whom the Lord uses powerfully. One piece of advice they gave was that after you experience a great time of ministry or something miraculous God has done, find time and retreat to your secret place. In your secret place, spend time thanking the Father for the miracle, His goodness and love for us. It's probably the most important advice I have heard. I've been used by God, and I never want Him to stop. In fact, I want Him to increase. What I know is true is that the spirit of pride is trailing close behind and wants to slip in and attach itself.

Going before our Father giving thanks and honor to Him soon after He displays miracles is the way to usher in the spirit of humility. It's rehearsing who we are in light of who He is. It gives pride no place to rest and it says to the Father we can be trusted with more. That's what being exalted means. Adopt this simple practice and welcome the more from the Father.

Learn from Jesus

Pride versus Humility

Proverbs 11:2 –
   Pride brings_____ Humility brings _____

James 4:6 –
   God _____the proud He gives _____ to the humble.

Proverbs 22:23 –
   Pride brings a person _____. A humble spirit obtains

   _____.

Live for Jesus

Read Philippians 2:8 and let Christ be your example as to what your attitude should be. For He, who had always been God by nature, **humbled Himself** by living a life of utter obedience.

Retreat to your secret place and ask the Lord what you must do to follow His example and humble yourself.

Love through Jesus (go and do)

In Matthew 5:16, Jesus says, "You are like that illuminating light. Let your light shine everywhere you go, that you may illumine creation, so men and women everywhere may see your good actions, may see creation at its fullest, may see your devotion to Me, and may turn and praise your Father in heaven because of it" (VOICE). **Go and do it!**

Today's Rhema Word – Week 7, Day 4

BREAK THE FLASK OF YOUR HEART

And being in Bethany at the house of Simon the leper, as He sat at the table, a woman came having an alabaster flask of very costly oil of spikenard. Then she broke the flask and poured it on His head.
(Mark 14:3 NKJV)

But the hour is coming, and now is, when the true worshipers will worship the Father in spirit and truth; for the Father is seeking such to worship Him.
(John 4:23 NKJV)

There are many who are holding back the alabaster bottle (flask) of their heart, withholding from our Father the true worship that is due Him. It's what the Father seeks. We are tasked to be leaders to set the atmosphere of worship in our families and our churches. All throughout scripture, worship involves our total being. It's expressive and full of life. David says let **everything** that has breath praise the Lord.

The woman with the alabaster flask could have opened the top of the flask and carefully poured the oil out in a controlled manner. No! She broke the flask and the oil poured out to demonstrate her extravagance in her worship toward the only One due our praise and honor. Break the flask of your heart and pour yourself out at the feet of King Jesus and worship Him extravagantly.

Learn from Worshippers of the Bible

Paul and Silas in Acts 16:24-28.

David in 2 Samuel 6:14.

How free are you in worship?

How comfortable are you in full-body worship?

Are you inhibited in your worship by what you feel others will think or say about you?

Live for Jesus

Jesus told the woman at the well, "true worshipers will worship the Father in spirit and truth."

Jesus said in Mark 12:30 you begin by

_____

_____

All throughout scripture worship involves our total being—body, soul, and spirit.

Love through Jesus (go and do)

In Psalm 150:6, David says, _____

Psalms 144-147 all begin with what phrase? _____

_____

These psalms describe how we can worship God in spirit and in truth. Implement what you have learned and worship Jesus in private then in public "for the Father is seeking such to worship Him."

Today's Rhema Word – Week 7, Day 5

PROPHETIC PRAISE WORSHIPPERS

Moreover David and the captains of the army separated for the service some of the sons of Asaph, of Heman, and of Jeduthun, who should prophesy with harps, stringed instruments, and cymbals.
(1 Chronicles 25:1 NKJV)

It is this company of prophetic praise worshipers that shall rip open the lid on God's awesome power. Beloved, may you join this company, and be a part of this end-time awakening. Be a man or woman who makes a difference. Allow the spirit of praise and worship to invade your life. Let it flow out of you in the bathroom, on your bed, in the kitchen, in your car, in your office, and on the street. Join this company that shall trigger the end-time revival.

While in the congregation of the saints, do not allow the myopic, stereotyped, lethargic, dull-beat spirit of worship in those around you to affect and nullify you. Rise up and affect them, let the spirit of praise and worship swell up inside of you, burst forth, gush out, and spill over. Change the atmosphere around you!

Let every hindrance of spiritual apathy and heaviness around you be broken up in Jesus' name.

Learn from Prophetic Praise Worshippers

What does 1 Chronicles 25:1 say these prophetic praise worshippers did as captains in David's army?

_____

In 2 Chronicles 20:21, what did Jehoshaphat do?

_____

Live for Jesus

Allow the spirit of praise and worship to invade your life. Let it flow out of you in the bathroom, on your bed, in the kitchen, in your car, in your office, and on the street, so you can rip open the lid on God's awesome power all throughout your day.

What steps do you need to take in order to make this happen in your life?

_____

_____

Love through Jesus (go and do)

Beloved, may you join this company of prophetic worshippers, and be a part of this end-time awakening. Be a man or woman who makes a difference in your world.

Will you accept the challenge?

Week 7, Day 6

HEARING & OBEYING GOD'S VOICE

REFLECTION QUESTIONS FOR YOU TO ANSWER THIS WEEK...

This week you learned about the strength of the joy of the Lord, the power of praise and worship in the lives of believers, and how to worship God in spirit and in truth as Jesus directed.

1. *How has what you learned this week changed your perspective on the importance and method of praising and worshipping God?*

   _____

   _____

   _____

2. *What have these lessons challenged you to do?*

   _____

   _____

   _____

3. *How did the lesson on pride and humility impact your life?*

   _____

   _____

   _____

"If there is a devil—and I believe there is—his work is to divide. If there is a Savior—and I believe there is—His work is to unite. It follows, therefore, that where division is, the devil is nearby. My proper response to division, then, is to disengage myself from whatever is causing it. If I would be on the side of the Redeemer, then I will do His work: I will engage in acts of reconciliation; I will become a peacemaker."

— Jean-Michel Hansen[15]

Today's Rhema Word – Week 8, Day 1

HIS PRESENCE AND POWER

"And these miracle signs will accompany those who believe:
They will drive out demons in the power of my name.
They will speak in tongues. They will be supernaturally protected
from snakes and from drinking anything poisonous.
And they will lay hands on the sick and heal them."
(Mark 16:17-18 TPT)

J esus told His disciples, "Go and preach the good news, and **then these miracle signs will accompany those who believe.**" I have been privileged to partner with the Holy Spirit on many occasions for healing the sick, casting out demons, speaking in tongues, and opening deaf ears. There are so many who preach God's Word and stop short of the demonstrations of His power. It's a lose-lose proposition. We lose out and we never get to share in the promise of Jesus. The hearer loses because they never get to have a supernatural encounter with the living God.

When people experience the power of God, they will never forget it. When things get tough and they doubt their salvation experience, they will always go back to the undeniable reality of His presence and power to keep them on track. His power is more than a sideshow, it's the main show. Do yourself and others a huge favor and show God's love in demonstrations of His power.

Learn from Jesus

Jesus told His disciples to:

Go _____

Then _____

And _____

Live for Jesus

Read 1 Corinthians 2:4 in several translations. Record how this verse encourages you to go and preach the good news as the Holy Spirit directs. Start with these.

Amplified Translation

_____

_____

Message Translation

_____

_____

Voice Translation

_____

_____

Love through Jesus (go and do)

Do yourself and others a huge favor and show God's love in demonstrations of His power. Pray and ask the Holy Spirit to direct you where to go to share the good news, and how to demonstrate the power of God's presence to minister to the needs of those He sends you to.

Today's Rhema Word – Week 8, Day 2

God's Sharpening and Shaping

*Then Jacob was left alone; and a Man wrestled with him until the
breaking of day. Now when He saw that He did not prevail against him,
He touched the socket of his hip; and the socket of Jacob's hip
was out of joint as He wrestled with him.
And He said, "Let Me go, for the day breaks."
But he said, "I will not let You go unless You bless me!"
So He said to him, "What is your name?" He said, "Jacob."
And He said, "Your name shall no longer be called Jacob, but Israel;
for you have struggled with God and with men,
and have prevailed."* (Genesis 32:24-28 NKJV)

Jacob was destined to become the leader of the twelve tribes of Israel but not in his current state. This is critical to understand. God can already see our calling and assignment. He also sees that our current state is not sufficient to accomplish His purposes. He uses divine circumstances to bring us into our purpose.

The key is that we are responsible to participate in the process. We must recognize God's sharpening and shaping and not resist what God is doing no matter how challenging or difficult. To quit is to let go of our destiny. Jacob recognized what God was doing. He refused to let go until his blessing was released. His name was changed from Jacob (to be behind) to Israel, meaning God prevails. I love Jacob's focus. He never took his eyes off the Lord.

Learn from Jesus

Don't resist what God is doing in your life no matter how challenging or difficult.

Describe an experience you now know was God sharpening and shaping you so you could move toward your destiny. Describe how you responded and what you learned.

_____

_____

_____

Live for Jesus

Read Jeremiah 18:1-4. Describe the Potter's Process.

_____

_____

_____

Love through Jesus (go and do)

How can you use what you have learned from the potter, Jacob, and your own experiences to help others understand God's sharpening and shaping so they will not resist God's process?

_____

_____

_____

Today's Rhema Word – Week 8, Day 3

REDEMPTION

"Agreed," she replied. "Let it be as you say." So she sent them away and they departed. And she tied the scarlet cord in the window. When they left, they went into the hills and stayed there three days, until the pursuers had searched all along the road and returned without finding them.
(Joshua 2:21-22 NIV)

The prostitute Rahab's faith was rewarded with the astounding honor of being placed in the genealogy of Jesus (Matthew 1:5) and being mentioned in the Hebrews 11 "Hall of Faith."

I had a vision of several demonic beings tied up in a lot of red cords (scarlet cords). The cords were charged with electricity and were bright red in appearance. The demonic beings were aggressively trying to break free but could not. Rahab's scarlet cord (Joshua 2:17,18; 6:17, 22-23) is a foretaste of how redemption will also come to faithful Gentiles like you and me.

It's a picture of what's happening in the spiritual realm as people are being set free to say yes to the King. Jesus' resurrection set in motion a freedom train for the whole earth to say YES to Him. Scarlet cords are being carried by the Heavenly hosts to bind up the spirits of darkness. Together with millions of believers all over the World, we celebrate the amazing freedom and future for all those being saved. Jesus is alive!

Learn from Jesus

Read Ephesians 1:7 and Hebrews 9:11 and use them to define redemption in Jesus:

_____

_____

_____

Live for Jesus

Our quote for this week suggests, "If I would be on the side of the Redeemer, then I will do His work: I will engage in acts of reconciliation; I will become a peacemaker."[16]

What acts of reconciliation came to mind when you read this?

_____

_____

Where are you being called to be a peacemaker?

_____

_____

Love through Jesus (go and do)

How would you explain redemption in Jesus to an unbeliever?

_____

_____

Today's Rhema Word – Week 8, Day 4

"It Is Finished!"

So when Jesus had received the sour wine, He said, "It is finished!"
And bowing His head, He gave up His spirit.
(John 19:30 NKJV)

Jesus was dead. He wasn't moving. They tested for signs of life by piercing His side. We often focus on His life and the glorious "getting up" morning as they say in the church, but what about His death? His death was meaningful and significant, too. As we die to our sin and self in Christ, we get to live with Him. In the book of James, he makes it clear that we all have sinned. He's not just talking past tense. It's present tense, too, because we currently are sinning.

We attended a Good Friday service and at the end of the service, we wrote on the paper the sins we were currently struggling with, whether "big or small." We walked to the front and nailed our sins to the cross. In the presence of the Father, we asked to be forgiven. After we nailed our sins to that cross, we walked away, not looking back.

It is finished!

His blood covers us once again so that we can live in His fullness. Take your sins afresh to the cross so you can live another day.

Learn from Jesus

✝If you have a cross on display in your home, take your sins and "nail" them to the cross. Ask God to forgive you and then take them down, rip them up, throw them away, and don't look back.

Declare, "It is finished!"

Live for Jesus

Read Colossians 2:9-15. List what it means to live in Him.
Verse 9
Verse 10
Verse 11
Verse 12
Verse 13
Verse 14
Verse 15

Love through Jesus (go and do)

Use Colossians 3:12-17 as your guide to love others through Jesus.

Especially focus on verses 16-17 which say,

_____

_____

_____

_____

Today's Rhema Word – Week 8, Day 5

"I Am He!"

And the moment Jesus spoke the words, "I am he,"
the mob fell backward to the ground! (John 18:6 TPT)

I've read the story of Jesus in the Garden of Gethsemane many times, but I've missed this small but significant detail in the story. The Garden was the last place of freedom Jesus experienced before His death, burial, and resurrection. It was the place where His humanity said, "I can't do it." The Spirit of God in His life said, "I can do it!" He surrendered His will to the will of the Father and prepared to meet His accusers and the betrayer of His soul.

Jesus asked them who they were looking for and they replied, Jesus of Nazareth. Jesus said, "I am He." It's the same phrase God spoke to Moses when asked who he should say sent him. God replied, "Tell them 'I Am' sent you." The Hebrews knew that phrase meant the self-existing one (Yahweh) GOD. The moment Jesus spoke these words, the mob fell to the ground under the power of God. Jesus could have fled, but He repeated Himself in total submission to the will of the Father.

What we want, what we feel or think, must bow before the King, the God of heaven and earth.

Learn from Jesus

Look deep inside, examine yourself, and make way for Heaven's will to manifest in and through you.

Is your will or the will of someone else in the way of the will of Father God in your life?

Live for Jesus

What we want, what we feel or think, must bow before the King, the God of heaven and earth.

Therefore, will you declare daily over your life, "Let Your Kingdom come, let Your will be done on earth as it is in Heaven?"

Love through Jesus (go and do)

To live and love through Jesus, we must be willing to submit to the will of the Father, just as Jesus did in the Garden. We begin by saying, "Not my will but Yours Father God," and then taking action to face whatever is trying to stand in our way as Jesus did.

Who or what do you need to face to move out in the will of God the Father?

_____

_____

Week 8, Day 6

HEARING & OBEYING GOD'S VOICE

REFLECTION QUESTIONS FOR YOU TO ANSWER THIS WEEK...

This week we discussed His Presence and Power and God's Sharpening and Shaping in our lives. Then we focused on Jesus' work on the cross.

1. *As a disciple of Jesus with a desire to serve Him with your life, how did these lessons help you tap more into the power and presence of God?*

   _____

   _____

2. God's process of sharpening and shaping is not always easy to submit to0.
   How did these lessons encourage you to stick with it and not quit until God moves you on?

   _____

   _____

3. *How have you been able to use what you have learned to help encourage others on their journey?*

   _____

   _____

4. *What new revelation did you receive through the additional study on Jesus' redemptive work on the cross?*

   _____

   _____

"Jesus said, 'The Kingdom of God is within' and 'I only say what I hear the Father saying and I only do what I see the Father doing'. Therefore, it is something we experience, articulate, and do. The Kingdom of God is already here but not yet fully realized."

— R. Alan Woods,
The Journey Is The Destination: A Photo Journal[17]

Today's Rhema Word – Week 9, Day 1

BLOOM WHERE YOU ARE PLANTED

May all believers continue to live the wonderful lives
God has called them to live,
according to what he assigns for each person,
for this is what I teach to believers everywhere.
(1 Corinthians 7:17 TPT emphasis added)

Recently I've been thinking about how the Lord grows us in our faith. Like a seed, He plants us in the soil of His vineyard. If we are paying attention, we will recognize His hand in the matter and know He has planted us in that place. Then, He creates the conditions for growth. Sometimes it's watering, while other times there is pruning. He will even fertilize to cause rapid growth and strength.

Wherever we find ourselves in the process, we can trust He knows what He is doing. There is the temptation to peek over into someone else's vineyard and admire their fields, but He calls us to stick it out and grow where we are planted.

In due season, He comes and carefully pulls us out of the ground, roots included, and transplants us into a new field. I remember Him doing that when we left Portland to move to Puerto Rico. I wasn't looking for it. He came to get me. No doubt there are other vineyards for all of us, but He will decide when we are ready for the transplant.

Learn from Jesus

Underline the key phrases Jesus spoke in John 15:1.

"I am the real vine, my Father is the vine-dresser. He removes any of my branches which are not bearing fruit and he prunes every branch that does bear fruit to increase its yield. Now, you have already been pruned by my words. You must go on growing in me and I will grow in you. For just as the branch cannot bear any fruit unless it shares the life of the vine, so you can produce nothing unless you go on growing in me. I am the vine itself, you are the branches. It is the man who shares my life and whose life I share who proves fruitful. For the plain fact is that apart from me you can do nothing at all. The man who does not share my life is like a branch that is broken off and withers away. He becomes just like the dry sticks that men pick up and use for the firewood. But if you live your life in me, and my words live in your hearts, you can ask for whatever you like and it will come true for you. This is how my Father will be glorified—in your becoming fruitful and being my disciples.[18]

Live for Jesus

"According to what he assigns for each person."

In due season, He comes and carefully pulls us out of the ground, roots included, and transplants us into a new field.

Are you being transplanted into a new field?

Do not resist. Seek to cooperate with the Vinedresser knowing He has a plan and a purpose for you in this new "location."

Love through Jesus (go and do)

Start to become more aware of your growth and that what you are learning and receiving is so you can be used by God as an instrument of blessing for those around you. Keep growing.

Keep a written or digital journal of what God is teaching you, how you are growing, and where He has transplanted you. Record how He uses you in your new location.

_____

_____

Today's Rhema Word – Week 9, Day 2

THE ANOINTING

Command the Israelites to bring you clear oil of pressed olives for the light so that the lamps may be kept burning.
(Exodus 27:20 NIV)

Not long ago, a quick image flashed before my eyes that appeared to be a black olive. Then, I saw a very large thumb and index finger begin to squeeze the olive like a press. As the olive was being squeezed, single drops of pure oil dripped from the olive on my head. It was a vision of oil that represents the anointing of the Holy Spirit. Not only within for our benefit, but the Holy Spirit upon us for the benefit of others. It was a vision of perpetual provision of His presence and an increase in our spiritual temperature and supernatural encounters with the living God.

We live amongst a generation of people who have heard the rhetoric and are exhausted by the cliches of religion. Now is the time when God will speak. His voice and presence will be undeniable. As we continually seek His face, we will witness His miracles, signs, and wonders. His presence will be piercing and permanent.

We thank You, Father, for allowing us to partner with You in this great end-time revival movement.

Receive from the Holy Spirit

Read 1 John 2:27 (AMP).

"As for you, the anointing [the special gift, the preparation] **which you received from Him** remains [permanently] in you, and you have no need for anyone to teach you. But just as His anointing teaches you [giving you insight through the presence of the Holy Spirit] about all things, and is true and is not a lie, and just as His anointing has taught you, you must remain in Him [being rooted in Him, knit to Him].

Describe and define the anointing of the Holy Spirit.

_____
_____
_____
_____

Prepare for Revival

The anointing of the Holy Spirit is not only within for our benefit, but also for the benefit of others. As we continually seek His face, we will witness His miracles, signs, and wonders. Read 2 Corinthians 5:20.

What are you called to be? _____

What does that mean you need to do? _____----_____

Partner with God (go and do)

Pray: *"We thank You, Father, for the anointing of the Holy Spirit and for allowing us to partner with You in this great end-time revival movement.*

Today's Rhema Word – Week 9, Day 3

THE SPOKEN WORD OF GOD

But He answered and said, "It is written, 'Man shall not live by bread alone, but by every word (Rhema) that proceeds from the mouth of God.'"
(Matthew 4:4 NKJV)

There are two Greek words in Scripture which are translated as "word" in the New Testament. *Logos* refers principally to the total inspired Word of God and to Jesus, Who is the living *Logos* (John 1:1, Luke 8:1, Philippians. 2:16, Hebrews 4:12).

Rhema is the Spoken Word of God. *Rhema* means an utterance. *Rhema* is a verse or portion of scripture the Holy Spirit brings to your attention with application to a current situation or need for direction for you or someone else (2 Timothy 3:16).

What do you do with a Rhema Word? First, you meditate on that word throughout the day. Ask the Holy Spirit to make that word a part of your spiritual DNA. Ask the Holy Spirit what to do with what the Word is saying.

Rhema comes from the Father's heart. Talk with the Holy Spirit about your next steps. He will let you know if some action is required.

Learn from the Holy Spirit

What do you do with a Rhema Word?

1. You meditate on that word throughout the day.
2. Ask the Holy Spirit to make that Word a part of your spiritual DNA.
3. Ask the Holy Spirit what to do with what the Word is saying.

Live for Jesus

Jesus said, *"Man shall not live by bread alone, but by every word (Rhema) that proceeds from the mouth of God."*

Living by God's Rhema word requires action.

You need to go and do what the Holy Spirit has told you to do. Talk with the Holy Spirit about your next steps. He will let you know if some action is required.

What is it the Holy Spirit is saying and wanting you to do?

_____

_____

Love through Jesus (go and do)

In Isaiah 55:11, God says, "So shall My word be that goes forth out of My mouth: it shall not return to Me void [without producing any effect, useless], but it shall accomplish that which I please *and* purpose, and it shall prosper in the thing for which I sent it."

Be a "Word-carrier" for Father God!

Today's Rhema Word – Week 9, Day 4

KINGDOM CULTURE

The LORD is in His holy temple, The LORD's throne is in heaven;
His eyes behold, His eyelids test the sons of men.
(Psalm 11:4 NKJV)

God's focus is on "who I am," not on "who I'm not." The world's focus is on "who I'm not, what I'm not doing, haven't accomplished, should have been, mistakes I've made, sin I've committed, and time I've lost." God sees us through the blood Jesus shed on the cross. As children of God, our Father sees what we shall become, all the great exploits we will do in His name, and all the great accomplishments we will make in partnership with Him. He sees us as holy because He is holy. He's excited we are redeeming the time and in step with His will.

Since that's how God sees us, we are obligated to see ourselves in the same way. God's ways are the superior reality. It doesn't mean the world doesn't exist. Jesus said we are in the world but not of the world. That means we live here, but our reality is shaped in Heaven by God. It's called Kingdom Culture.

We are here on assignment.
The world doesn't define us, Heaven defines us.
No matter what surrounds you today,
begin to see yourself through God's eyes.
See Yourself from God's Perspective

If you are a born-again believer, what does the Bible say God's perspective is of you? (See Romans 8:16-17, Philippians 3:20, Galatians 3:13 Ephesians 1:6, John 16:27, 1 Peter 1:16.)

_____

_____

Live for Jesus

Define the world's vision of you: _____

_____

Define God's vision: _____

_____

You can't live under two different visions.

Which do you choose? _____

Love through Jesus (go and do)

We are here on assignment as Christ's ambassador (2 Corinthians 5:29).

Look up and list the duties and responsibilities of an ambassador.

_____

_____

_____

Today's Rhema Word – Week 9, Day 5

OPEN HEAVEN

"Go and gather together all the Jews of Susa and fast for me. Do not eat or drink for three days, night or day. My maids and I will do the same. And then, though it is against the law, I will go in to see the king. If I must die, I am willing to die."
(Esther 4:16 NLT)

The Holy Spirit asked me if I would be willing to give my life for this one thing. He said there was something important God wanted me to share with His people—the reality of the "Open Heaven." Throughout scripture we see the God of the universe stepping out of Heaven to come to earth and reveal Himself and Heaven's agenda. He talks about "Rending" the heavens (Isaiah 64:1). We see a vision of a ladder where angels are ascending and descending from Heaven to earth and the veil to the Holy of Holies being torn at the crucifixion of Jesus. More importantly, we read the Apostolic prayer of Jesus in Matthew 6:10, "Your kingdom come, Your will be done on earth as it is in heaven."

Through intimacy with the Holy Spirit, we have access to Heaven's resources. The Father asked me if I would be willing to live, demonstrate, and share this one thing, no matter what. I committed to doing just that, making it my pursuit and my passion.

How about you?

Learn from Jesus

Perhaps you have prayed the "Lord's Prayer" without really focusing on what each part means for us as disciples of Jesus and members of His kingdom. It appears at first glance we are asking our Heavenly Father to do these things for us. However, each part involves us as well. Praying Matthew 6:10, "Your kingdom come, Your will be **done** on earth as it is in heaven," requires willing participants to accomplish it. To get something **done**, someone has to **do** something.

Live for Jesus

James 1:22 says, "But be doers of the word, and not hearers only, deceiving yourselves" (NKJV). The Father asked me if I would be willing to live, demonstrate, and share this one thing, no matter what.

*What is God asking you to be willing to **do** with your life?*

I committed to **do**ing just that, making it my pursuit and my passion. *What is He showing you that can become your pursuit and passion?*

Love through Jesus (go and do)

Through intimacy with the Holy Spirit, we have access to Heaven's resources so we can **go and do** what He is asking us to **do**. Pray and ask the Holy Spirit to reveal your mission and how to access the heavenly resources to **go and do it**.

Week 9, Day 6

HEARING & OBEYING GOD'S VOICE

REFLECTION QUESTIONS FOR YOU TO ANSWER THIS WEEK...

This was an incredibly powerful week as we studied Blooming Where You Are Planted, The Anointing, Rhema-The Spoken Word of God, Kingdom Culture, and manifesting Matthew 6:10 on the earth. "Your kingdom come, Your will be done on earth as it is in heaven."

1. These topics may have seemed unrelated to each other, but in truth, you need to understand each concept to be able to complete the mission of Matthew 6:10.

    Which day brought you the most impactful revelation and why?

    _____

    _____

2. *Which day brought the most changes in your life?*

    _____

    _____

3. *What goals have you set for yourself to move you along God's plan and purpose for your life?*

    _____

    _____

"The glory of God isn't just a feeling, an event or an Old Testament experience—it's a spiritual tsunami of everything contained in the character of God."
— Kenneth Copeland[19]

Today's Rhema Word – Week 10, Day 1

INVITE HIM IN

When I remember You on my bed, I meditate on
You in the night watches.
(Psalm 63:6 NKJV)

Literally, Jesus' name is the last word on my lips before I go to sleep at night. After I finish praying with my wife, I give her a kiss goodnight. I turn over and give my final words to my King, Savior, Redeemer, Deliverer, Healer, and Father. I tell Him how much I love Him. I thank Him again for walking with me. Finally, I invite Him into my dream world. He is my first and my last thought each day.

It's truly a love affair. It's a wonderful thing, not a religious thing to live with Jesus 24/7 365.

Try focusing on His presence all day.

Start in the morning.

Check in with Him throughout the day.

End with Him at night.

If you're blessed, He will come to you in your dreams.

Invite Him In

Begin your day with prayer: *Father, thank You that I can come to You at the beginning of each day and invite Your presence into my life. Holy Spirit, I ask You to guide me throughout my day. I thank You, Jesus, for Your love that fills my mind and gives me peace as I sleep.*

Learn From Paul How to Live for Jesus

To Truly Live for Jesus We Must…

- ➤ Trust and submit to God's Plan (Read Galatians 2:20).
- ➤ Exalt Him in everything we do (Read Philippians 1:20).
- ➤ Focus on discipleship (Read Philippians 2:12-16).

Love through Jesus (go and do)

Paul said, "And if the Spirit of him who raised Jesus from the dead is living in you, he who raised Christ from the dead will also give life to your mortal bodies because of his Spirit who lives in you" (Romans 8:11).

Now Go and Do what He has called you to do!

SEEK TO EXPERIENCE HIS GLORY

*Eight days later, Jesus took Peter, James, and John
And climbed a high mountain to pray. **As he prayed**,
his face began to glow until it was a blinding glory streaming from him.
His entire body was illuminated with a radiant glory.
His brightness became so intense that it made his clothing
blinding white, like multiple flashes of lightning.*
(Luke 9:28-29 TPT)

Every time we get alone with Jesus, we want to see His glory. There are times when our time alone seems very ordinary, but just on the other side of the ordinary is His glory waiting to be revealed to us if we will contend for it.

When I go away with Him, He comes to me and reveals Himself in different ways. Sometimes, it is so overwhelming that I break down in tears. Other times, I'm in awe of the visions He reveals. Yet other times, I'll hear His still small voice whispering words of life to me. There are times that the heavenly language of the Holy Spirit will come bubbling up in unceasing worship.

There's something about getting alone with the Father that calls His attention to us. Jesus took three of His closest disciples with Him because He wanted them to experience His glory. His glory is only found in the context of intimacy with Him.

Seek to Experience His Glory.

Experiencing His Glory

Read Exodus 33:12-23.

*How did Moses' life change after this encounter with the
Glory of God?*

_____

_____

Read Acts 7:54-60.

How was Saul's life impacted after witnessing this event?

_____

_____

Live for Jesus

*Though Jesus is the Son of God, what was the first thing He did after they
climbed up that mountain?* _____

Describe a time when you experienced His glory:

_____

_____

Love through Jesus (go and do)

*Now the Lord is the Spirit, and where the Spirit of the Lord is, there is
freedom. And we all, who with unveiled faces contemplate the Lord's
glory, are being transformed into his image with ever-increasing glory,
which comes from the Lord, who is the Spirit.*
(2 Corinthians 3:17-18 NIV)

Allow the Lord's glory to transform you into His image so you can go
and fulfill your destiny.

REVIVAL IS COMING!

Oh, that You would rend the heavens! That You would come down!
That the mountains might shake at Your presence.
(Isaiah 64:1 NKJV)

The message of Isaiah 64 is that revival can come to us at any time if we get right with God, band together and pray, and put ourselves at God's disposal. R.A. Torrey said, "I have a theory…that there is not a church, chapel, or mission on earth where you cannot have revival, provided there is a little nucleus of faithful people who will hold onto God until He comes down."

First, let a few Christians—there need not be many—get thoroughly right with God themselves. This is the prime essential. If this is not done, the rest cannot be done, and it will come to nothing.

Second, let them bind themselves together to pray for revival until God opens the heavens and comes down.

Third, let them put themselves at the disposal of God to use them as He sees fit in winning others to Christ. That's all. This is sure to bring revival to any church, any community, anywhere!

I have given this prescription around the world. It has been taken by many churches and many communities, and in no instance has it ever failed, and it cannot fail."[20]

Revival is coming!

Learn from R. A. Torrey

First, let a few Christians get thoroughly right with God themselves. This is the prime essential. If this is not done, the rest, I'm sorry to say, cannot be done, and it will come to nothing."

Once this is done, move on to step two.

Step Two

"Second, let them bind themselves together to pray for revival until God opens the heavens and comes down. I have given this prescription around the world."

Step Three (go and do)

"Third, let them put themselves at the disposal of God to use them as He sees fit in winning others to Christ."

We don't have to persuade God to send revival, we only have to permit Him to do so. The message of Isaiah 64 is that revival can come to us at any time if we get right with God, band together and pray, and put ourselves at God's disposal. Let's do it!

Today's Rhema Word – Week 10, Day 4

THE SOUND OF REVIVAL

*Blessed are the people **who know the joyful sound!***
They walk, O LORD, in the light of Your countenance.
(Psalm 89:15 NKJV)

There is a closeness we must have with the Lord. He is coming to our town. Revival is just a stone's throw away. It's not far off. *Do you know the sound? Do you know what revival sounds like? Will you recognize its sounds?* I'm anxiously waiting and preparing myself for His coming. He asked Lisa and me to help prepare a people who are hungry for more of Him, who know there is more, crave the more, and want to walk with the Father in His light. They have forsaken the darkness and opened every part of their souls to the brilliant and radiant light of Jesus. It is these sons and daughters who will recognize the sound. Revival has a sound.

Though I've never been a part of a modern-day revival, I do consider myself a revivalist. I've studied many revival movements and learned revival has a sound. It's a sound that is undeniable. It's facilitated by the Holy Spirit. When we hear it, the call is to partner with it. We anxiously await the generous outpouring of the Holy Spirit. He's coming. Prepare yourself through deep intimacy with the Father.

This next awakening is going to change everything!

Learn from Those Who Know the Sound

Do you know what revival sounds like?

How will you recognize its sound?

Those who know have forsaken the darkness and opened every part of their soul to the brilliant and radiant light of Jesus. These are the sons and daughters who will recognize the sound. You need to become one and connect with others of the same mind like those who were praying in the upper room on the day of Pentecost in Acts 2.

Prepare for Revival

Jesus' disciples are always preparing for revival through deep intimacy with the Father. After those first disciples were filled with the Holy Spirit on the day of Pentecost, a great revival began with the first sermon Peter ever preached. Prepare for revival.

Read Acts 2:5-24.

Partner with the Holy Spirit (go and do)

Revival has a sound. It's a sound that is undeniable. It's facilitated by the Holy Spirit like that sound that filled the upper room in Acts 2:2. When we hear it, the call is to partner with it. Be ready!

**This next awakening is going
to change everything.**

Today's Rhema Word – Week 10, Day 5

HUNGER FOR "THE MORE" OF HIM

Moreover, I will give you what you have not asked for—both riches and honor—so that in your lifetime you will have no equal among kings.
(1 Kings 3:13 NIV)

This is a promise we live under. He has more for us. More is not what we ask for. More is what He has for us that we haven't asked for. We don't even know what to ask.

Now to Him Who, by (in consequence of) the [action of His] power that is at work within us, is able to [carry out His purpose and] do superabundantly, far over and above all that we [dare] ask or think [infinitely beyond our highest prayers, desires, thoughts, hopes, or dreams]. (Ephesians 3:20 AMPC)

I'm excited because "the more" is upon us. "The more" will be like glimpses of opportunities that He invites us into. The secret to more of God is a *hunger* for more of Him!

"Blessed [joyful, nourished by God's goodness] are those who hunger and thirst for righteousness [those who actively seek right standing with God], for they will be [completely] satisfied.
(Matthew 5:6 AMP)

**Time to hunger and thirst for His way
as we actively seek Him.**

Learn from Jesus

Jesus taught the secret to more of God in Matthew 5:6.

What is the definition Jesus gave for "blessed" in the Amplified translation of Matthew 5:6? _____

How do you attain this blessing? _____

What do you receive if you do this? _____

Live for Jesus

Use the following scriptures to define how to live a life of righteousness and achieve the more of God.

James 1:19-20

_____

_____

Romans 13:11-14

_____

_____

Love through Jesus (go and do)

Jesus taught an interesting truth about giving to the needy and receiving more from God in Matthew 6:1-4. *How has this truth helped you show God's love through giving of yourself, your talents, and your resources to others?*

_____

_____

Week 10, Day 6

HEARING & OBEYING GOD'S VOICE

REFLECTION QUESTIONS FOR YOU TO ANSWER THIS WEEK...

This week brought us powerful revelations about understanding and **Seeking to Experience His Glory** and be in preparation because a **Revival Is Coming that is going to change everything!**

1. *As you completed your studies this week, what is the underlying theme of experiencing God's glory and preparing for the coming revival?*

    _____

    _____

    _____

2. *What life-impacting keys did you discover this week?*

    _____

    _____

    _____

3. *How are you going to help others prepare for what God is getting ready to do on the earth?*

    _____

    _____

    _____

"When you know how much God is in love with you then you can only live your life radiating that love."

— Mother Teresa, "A Simple Path"[21]

Today's Rhema Word – Week 11, Day 1

GIFTING VERSUS CHARACTER

If I were to speak with eloquence in earth's many languages,
and in the heavenly tongues of angels, yet I didn't express myself
with love, my words would be reduced to the hollow sound
of nothing more than a clanging cymbal.
(1 Corinthians 13:1 TPT)

Paul is addressing something often overlooked in our churches today: gifting versus character. God prefers character above talent or ability. God gives spiritual gifts to His sons and daughters freely. We don't earn them.

Character, in this case, love, is a fruit of the Spirit. Love is born out of a relationship with Jesus. Jesus left us with a simple commandment that encompasses all of the Old Covenant commandments. Love God with everything we are and love our neighbor as ourselves.

Paul speaks candidly and says if we're gifted and talented but it's not about love, then we sound like the guy in the marching band with the big cymbals clanging them together as loud as possible. Super annoying! In our ministries, with all of the gifting we have, the sound that resonates sweetly in our Father's ear is love. The love of the Father is designed to flow like a river in and through us. Let it flow!

Learn from the Apostle Paul

Read 1 Corinthians 12:11b.

What is Paul saying he wants to teach us? _____

Ask Yourself...
Do I "blow my own horn" when about spiritual gifts? _____

Do I sound like the guy in the marching band with the big cymbals clanging them together as loud as possible? _____

What sound resonates sweetest in my Father's ear? _____

What is the difference in these two sounds according to Paul?

_____

Paul's Lesson Part Two

Read the rest of Paul's lesson in 1 Corinthians 13:2-3.

Verse 2 says:

_____

_____

Verse 3 says

_____

_____

Now read 1 Corinthians 13:11.

What do you need to do? _____

Love through Jesus (go and do)

Our life in Christ should be a love letter to the world.

In every environment that we serve, let's pause and ask ourselves:

Am I about love? _____ *Do I have a high love quotient (capacity for loving others)?* _____

Today's Rhema Word – Week 11, Day 2

SET YOUR AFFECTIONS ABOVE

Moreover, because I have set my affection on the house of my God, I have given to the house of my God, over and above all that I have prepared for the holy house, my own special treasure of gold and silver:
(1 Chronicles 29:3 NKJV)

My wife recently heard a prophecy about an upcoming out-pouring of the Holy Spirit in our country. The prophecy was focused on individuals, saying readiness is required.

Was she talking about knowing the scriptures and reaching out to those who are waiting to be found?

No, she was talking about when God pours out His Spirit on us, the enemy will do whatever he can to crush that move of God through our affections. If we have any desires connected to something that's not godly, it will be used against us no matter how small.

I immediately went to the Father and began searching my heart using Psalm 51. The Holy Spirit began showing me things that seemed small, but under pressure would become huge issues. Check your affections and make sure they are squarely placed on Jesus.

Learn from Psalm 51

Read Psalm 51. Check your affections and make sure they are squarely placed on Jesus.

What has the Holy Spirit revealed to you about the condition of your heart?

_____

_____

Learn from Paul in Colossians Chapter 3

Read Colossians 3:2-4.

What kinds of things consume your thoughts?

Money	Technology	Food	Entertainment
Travel	Clothing	Sports	Television

Other_____

Read Colossians 3:12-14.

What are the godly things above you should be focusing on?

_____

_____

Love through Jesus (go and do)

Read Colossians 3:15-17.

Your goals and affections should not be set on the things in the earth but to please your heavenly Father above in Heaven

What are your goals now based on what you have learned?

_____

_____

Today's Rhema Word – Week 11, Day 3

CHRISTIAN CELEBRITY SYNDROME

So Samuel said, "When you were little in your own eyes,
were you not head of the tribes of Israel? And did not the LORD
anoint you king over Israel?"
(1 Samuel 15:17 NKJV)

Samuel the Prophet is recounting Saul's rejection as king. Saul was the people's choice. They wanted a king and God anointed Saul in great ways. However, somewhere along the way Saul started to "feel himself and read his own press." That's when things started going downhill.

God will test you when He moves powerfully on your life. He waits to see if your heart changes, your chest puffs out, your head gets big. You have to avoid the "Christian Celebrity Syndrome." That's when God uses you in cool ways and those around you begin to sing your praises more than they sing the praises of Jesus. If you don't course correct, usually, some sort of fall follows.

God is looking for you to remember we are all like grains of sand on the seashore. It's an honor the King of Glory would use you to do His exploits. Keep it in perspective. Stay away from your own press.

Learn from the Mistakes of Others

The "Christian Celebrity Syndrome" has caused the fall of biblical leaders as well as modern-day ministers.

Read some of Saul's history and where he began to "read his own press" in 1 Samuel 9:17, 10:6, 13:1-10, 1 Samuel 13:11-12.

What did Samuel tell him caused his removal as the leader of God's people? (1 Samuel 13:13-14.) _____

What did God say about Saul to Samuel? (1 Samuel 15:10-10, 26.)

The Body of Christ

Remember you are **not** a one-man or one-woman show. You are an important part of the body of Christ, but you must always work together with all the other "parts" for the common good.

Read 1 Corinthians 12:4-6, 12-27.

What happens to the "body" when one part of the body thinks it is more important than another part? _____

Keep Your Eyes on Jesus (go and do)

Stay away from your own press and keep your heart and eyes on Jesus. Great things are coming your way as you go and do His exploits.

Today's Rhema Word – Week 11, Day 4

QUIET YOUR HEART BEFORE GOD

"Be still, and know that I am God..."
(Psalm 46:10a NKJV)

When there's lots of stuff swirling in your personal world, that's the time to stop everything, close your eyes, and feel the presence of your Father. Being with Him is like going back to being a little child when you had no cares in the world. You know everything is going to be okay. In the stillness, you become aware of His greatness.

**There is something very tangible and powerful about
quieting your heart before God.**

When you stop what you're doing and turn all your attention to the Father, let Him carry your vision into His throne room. He loves to spend time with His children! **Enjoy your Heavenly Father today.**

Time spent with Him in silence strips us of the striving and brings us into a deeper place of peace and trust. New thoughts will emerge, new ideas will surface, and new direction becomes clear.

Learn from Your Father

Stop what you're doing, find a quiet space, and turn all your attention to the Father. Let Him carry your vision into His throne room.

Look around.

What's He doing? _____

What's He saying to you? _____

Enjoy Your Father Today

Being with Him is like going back to being a little child when you had no cares in the world. In the stillness, you become aware of His greatness.

How do you feel being with Him?

_____

_____

Instructions From the Father (go and do)

New thoughts emerge, new ideas surface, and new direction becomes clear when you spend time with Him in silence so you can go and do His will.

What new thoughts, ideas, and directions did you receive?

_____

_____

Today's Rhema Word – Week 11, Day 5

JESUS PURSUES AND RESTORES

Therefore that disciple whom Jesus loved said to Peter,
"It is the Lord!" Now when Simon Peter heard that it was the Lord,
he put on his outer garment (for he had removed it),
and plunged into the sea. (John 21:7 NKJV)

After Peter had denied Jesus, he was depressed and discouraged and walked away from following Jesus to return to fishing. When Jesus showed Himself after His resurrection, He went to find Peter and call him back to following Him.

Many who have been wounded of soul feel the Lord is disappointed in them when, in reality, He is still pursuing them like He did Peter. The love of Jesus pursues us. It never leaves us where we are.

God unleashes the hounds of Heaven, and they don't stop until they find us. That's what His love does for each one of His sons and daughters. Once He finds us, He fully restores us until we are exactly what He designed us to be. Let's celebrate His amazing love for us today.

The love of the Father doesn't stop until His work is complete in us.

Jesus Reinstates Peter

Read John 21:15-17.

What three questions did Jesus ask Peter? _____

How did Peter answer each question? _____

What did Jesus tell Peter to go and do? _____

Love as Jesus Loves

In the Hebrew language, there are three words translated as love. Jesus used the word *agape* when asking the first two questions. *Agape* means unconditional, sacrificial love (no strings attached). Peter used the word *phileo* when he answered Jesus' questions which means brotherly friendship.

What was Jesus trying to get Peter to understand as He commissioned him to "feed my sheep"?

_____

_____

Love through Jesus (go and do)

Jesus has commissioned us to also "feed My sheep." *How is He calling us to love as we lead and disciple others?*

_____

_____

Week 11, Day 6

Hearing & Obeying God's Voice

Reflection Questions for You to Answer This Week...

> "I'm a little pencil in the hand of a writing God,
> who is sending a love letter to the world."
> — Mother Teresa[22]

This week was basically about gaining a deeper understanding of God's agape love for us and through us to others.

1. Love is born out of a relationship with Jesus. Jesus left us with two simple commandments.

   What are those commandments?

   _____

   _____

2. Mother Teresa said our lives in Christ should be love letters to the world.

   Is that how you would describe your life?

   If no, what changes have you found you need to make?

   _____

   _____

"Christ's invitation to the weary and heavy-laden is a call to begin life over again upon a new principle--upon His own principle. 'Watch My way of doing things,' He says. 'Follow Me. Take life as I take it. Be meek and lowly, and you will find Rest.'"

— Henry Drummond[23]

Today's Rhema Word – Week 12, Day 1

"I Am Not the Christ"

John answered and said, "A man can receive nothing unless it has been given to him from heaven. You yourselves bear me witness, that I said, 'I am not the Christ,' but, 'I have been sent before Him.'"
(John 3:27-28 NKJV)

They were longing for someone to believe in, someone to connect with, and John the Baptist was that guy. In all of our relationships, we long for deep connections, fathers to children, wives to husbands, husband to wives, and friend to friend. The challenge in all relationships is that there is something inside of us that aches for more. The mistake we make is we seek it in our human relationships, but it puts both parties in an awkward place. What we are seeking is something that can only be satisfied by Jesus.

We set ourselves up for disappointment when we desire from a human relationship what only Jesus can give us. He provides the deeper things no one else can provide and should not try. It takes the pressure off and allows us to pursue relationships in a healthy and God-honoring way.

Allow Heaven's love to fill in the cracks and make all the difference in your earthly relationships.

Learn from John the Baptist

John knew what his mission was, just like Jesus knew what His mission was while on the earth. When we are secure in who God has called us to be, we do not need others to give us the security and peace only Jesus can provide.

What was John to do? _____

*What was John **not** supposed to do?* _____

Why is that important for you to understand in your earthly relationships and ministry?

_____

_____

Live for Jesus

Read John 1:26-27, 29, 34.

What did John clearly declare? _____

How could he have known this? _____

What do you need to do to have your relationships in order so you can truly live for Jesus?

_____

_____

Love through Jesus (go and do)

The challenge in all relationships is that there is something inside of us that aches for more.

What is the only way to fill that void? _____

When you do, it will make all the difference in your earthly relationships.

Today's Rhema Word – Week 12, Day 2

DELIVERANCE

When the LORD brought back the captivity of Zion,
We were like those who dream. Then our mouth was filled with laughter,
And our tongue with singing. Then they said among the nations,
"The LORD has done great things for them."
(Psalm 126:1-2 NKJV)

Deliverance is when the soul is cleansed and emptied of all the junk we have carried, and we're opened up to a whole new world of possibility. We become like those who dream. Thoughts of our future and hope for what God wants for our lives will flow without effort. It's like all of life is brand new. The air never smelled so good. The trees never looked so green. The sounds were never so clear. It's like a "do-over" in life and spontaneous laughter flows from within.

The children of Israel spent large portions of their lives in captivity. They had lost sight of the God of their forefathers and their spiritual inheritance. Then, at that moment accompanying their deliverance, they suddenly realized the world was their playground and nothing was impossible.

Dream, think about the possibilities, and allow Jesus to carry you into your destiny.

Learn from Children of Israel

The children of Israel spent large portions of their lives in captivity causing them to lose sight of their spiritual inheritance.

What has your "captivity" been that has caused you to lose sight of your spiritual inheritance? _____

What junk do you need to get rid of?

_____

_____

Live for Jesus

Deliverance can open up a whole new world of possibility. Keep a journal of how your life begins to change as you allow Jesus to carry you into your destiny.

_____

_____

Love through Jesus (go and do)

Then they said among the nations, "The LORD has done great things for them."

Is this what is happening in your life? _____

If not, what do you need to do right away?

_____

_____

_____

Today's Rhema Word – Week 12, Day 3

GOD'S WONDERS

Stephen, who was a man full of grace and supernatural power,
performed many astonishing signs and wonders and
mighty miracles among the people.
(Acts 6:8 TPT)

Stephen was not an apostle, yet God displayed signs and wonders through his ministry. God's wonders are not for the few but for the many. The Greek Word for "wonders" is *téras* – a miraculous wonder, done to elicit a reaction from onlookers; an extraordinary event with its supernatural effect left on all witnessing it.[24]

I recently watched the movie *Mary Poppins Returns*. It was full of wonders. Unfortunately, the world has hijacked the realm of wonders. The greatest wonders belong to our God.

I was in Mexico when some difficult news came my way. I was on the phone with the airline changing my ticket when I looked up and about a hundred feet above me, thirty to forty black-colored birds were circling. Birds like that circle when death is near. I sensed something demonic toward me. In a whisper, I commanded the birds to disperse. One by one, the birds flew in different directions until they had all disappeared. Our Father is ready to reveal Himself and draw praise from us and anyone observing.

Learn from Stephen's Ministry

Though he was not an apostle, what does Acts 6:8 say Stephen was that qualified him to perform many astonishing signs, wonders, and mighty miracles among the people? _____

_____

Are you experiencing these manifestations in your life? _____

Pray and ask the Holy Spirit what you need to do to achieve this.

Live for Jesus

Unfortunately, the world has hijacked the realm of wonders. Modern technology has produced "wonders" that captivate our young people and distract and disillusion them from turning to God. Begin your day asking God how you can be a living example of His wonders, especially to the young people in your life.

Love through Jesus (go and do)

The Greek Word for "wonders" is *téras* – a miraculous wonder, done to elicit a reaction from onlookers; an extraordinary event with its supernatural effect left on all witnessing it.[25] Become the "Stephen" in your area of influence so that those around you will see and desire to know God, the creator of the wonders He does through you.

Today's Rhema Word – Week 12, Day 4

ENTER HIS REST

Now God has offered to us the same promise of entering into his realm of resting in confident faith. So we must be extremely careful to ensure that we all embrace the fullness of that promise and not fail to experience it.
(Hebrews 4:1 TPT)

For many, rest is like taking a break from everything you are doing and doing nothing. That's not exactly what the author of Hebrews is getting at in this passage.

There is a place in our relationship with Jesus when we begin to live in total trust. There is a confidence inside of us that He's got this. He's dialed into our life and is in direction mode. That's the place of rest He's promised us. It's not a place of inactivity like resting in the natural. It's actually in between doing and trusting. All our fears, concerns, apprehensions, and worries are washed away. In their place, the Holy Spirit takes over and leaves us with assignments, tasks, directives, nudges, and inspirations. We pick up on all His cues and we simply follow His lead. That's the promise that can only be accessed by learning to "rest in Him."

Lean into the Holy Spirit and watch Him take over. It's crazy! It won't be like you think, but you can totally trust in Him.

Learn to Embrace the Promise

This is a good time to learn to seek God's promise for whatever you are going through in your life. Begin by memorizing the promises you need right now in your life. Start by memorizing and declaring Proverbs 3:5-6.

Do you need healing? Memorize and declare Jeremiah 17:14.

Do you need wisdom? Memorize and declare James 3:17.

Live for Jesus

"We must be extremely careful to ensure that we all embrace the fullness of that promise and not fail to experience it."

Take a look at your life and ask yourself the question, *What do I need to do now to enter into His rest?*

Then practice the promise you have memorized.

Lean into the Holy Spirit and watch Him take over.

Love through Jesus (go and do)

Read Psalm 37:3-7. To enter God's rest requires action. These verses give us the action required.

Verse 3 says, _____

Verse 4 says, _____

Verse 5 says, _____

Verse 7 says, _____

Now go and do.

Today's Rhema Word – Week 12, Day 5

ANCHOR OF THE SOUL

This hope we have as an anchor of the soul, both sure and steadfast, and which enters the Presence behind the veil.
(Hebrews 6:19 NKJV)

The Holy Spirit led me to this scripture after a conversation I had with my neighbor who is still "waiting to be found (unsaved)." He wants to give his son a vehicle. He's a high school junior. His challenge is that his son wants to smoke weed and party. So, his dad made him a deal. Monday through Friday, if he gets good grades and no partying, he will give his son a vehicle. On the weekends, he could go ahead and party. That was their deal. That's what life looks like without the anchor that keeps us in place.

Life without Jesus is anchorless. That means anything goes. Not only does the anchor keep us tethered to God's heart and His value system, but it also gives us access to His limitless power!

My neighbor may feel pressured to broker such an unwise deal with his son because he feels powerless. I thank Jesus for the anchor of our soul and the unprecedented access to Heaven's resources. My neighbor is close to discovering the Anchor for his soul. He mentioned he has almost finished reading a book I gave him several months ago called "*The Case for Christ,*" by Lee Strobel.

Learn from Jesus

Our spiritual anchor keeps us grounded on what matters most so we are able to cope with the challenges of life.

Read Hebrews 4:14-16.

List the reasons Jesus is the anchor of our soul.

_____

_____

Live for Jesus

Define anchor: _____

What does an anchor symbolize? _____

What does it mean to you to be anchored in Jesus?

_____

_____

Love through Jesus (go and do)

"Leaders who really know their values, the ones that never change, find they serve as an anchor in a crisis." – Eric Norwood[26]

How are you serving as an anchor in a crisis for others in your area of influence?

_____

_____

Week 12, Day 6

HEARING & OBEYING GOD'S VOICE

T his week we learned not only about God's rest but how to enter His rest. We also discovered our spiritual anchor keeps us grounded on what matters most so we're able to cope with the challenges of life and become leaders for those around us who may be facing a crisis in their lives.

1. *Why is entering His rest so important as we prepare to enter the mission field He has called us to on our life's journey?*

   _____

   _____

   _____

2. *What have you discovered this week that is an important part of being a Christian leader to your family, friends, co-workers, and neighbors?*

   _____

   _____

   _____

"When the breakthrough comes it erases the weariness of the previous season, a refreshing presence of the Lord comes upon you, and you know that the waiting was worth the outcome result."

— James W. Goll[27]

Today's Rhema Word – Week 13, Day 1

REPARATION

The heart of her husband safely trusts her;
So he will have no lack of gain.
She does him good and not evil all the days of her life.
(Proverbs 31:11-12 NKJV)

"You have to behave your way back to trust," from *The Speed of Trust* by Stephen Covey.[28]

What a profound statement!

Trust is demonstrated not just with words but with actions. When relationships are broken, trust must be repaired. It's like reparation. Reparation is a legal term for going back and righting a wrong. Fixing what we've messed up is very biblical. It's the final step of forgiveness. Blessing those who have hurt us or those whom we have hurt is an important part of the reparation.

It's like a bridge that has been damaged. If you want to get to the other side again, you have to repair it. Simply put, it's repaired by our behavior. It's not just what we say, it's what we *do* and say that communicates to the other person, "I want you to trust me." If all your relationships are good at the moment, praise Jesus. If a time comes when a relationship mending is in order, this process will come in handy. Now you have the secret sauce.

Learn from Jesus

Fixing what we've messed up is very biblical. It's the final step of forgiveness.

Read what Jesus said in Matthew 6:14-15.

Do you have a relationship that needs mending? _____

What are the two ingredients to the secret sauce?

_____

_____

Live Like Jesus

We will hurt others and others will hurt us but dwelling on wrongs and refusing to let them go can cause angry division, emotional instability, and painful separation in our relationships.

Proverbs 17:9 says, "He who covers over an _____ promotes _____, but whoever _____ the matter _____ close _____" (NIV).

Love through Jesus (go and do)

When relationships are broken, trust must be repaired.

Read what Jesus tells us in Matthew 18:15.

What do you need to do if there is a someone who has hurt you?

_____

Why is this so important as you seek to love through Jesus?

_____

Go and do and win back a friend!

Today's Rhema Word – Week 13, Day 2

WATCH FOR STRANGE FRUIT

"...making the word of God of no effect through your
tradition which you have handed down.
And many such things you do."
(Jesus in Mark 7:13 NKJV)

Since we now can travel all over the world and are exposed to various streams of Christian ministry, it is no surprise Christians have mixed many of their own personal and cultural ideas and traditions with the Word of God.

This mixing can produce "strange fruit" in the body of Christ. *How do you know?* You must know the Word for yourself. If what you see happening is not producing the fruit of the Spirit, which is our indicator of growing intimacy with the Father, then it could indeed be a "strange fruit" and will not be pleasing to God.

Jesus warned us to make a clear distinction between what culture says and what God is saying. Culture will change, but God's Word remains the same. God's Word is meant to inform and transform culture, not the other way around.

Let's be responsive to the culture and faithful
in making His Word relevant for today.

Learn from Jesus

What kind of "traditions" have you witnessed in churches or ministries that make you wonder what God thinks about them?

_____

_____

What "strange fruit" have you discovered as a result of some of these "traditions"?

_____

_____

Live for Jesus

Read the Message Translation of Romans 12:2. Notice the progression the warning takes.

1. "**Don't** become so well-adjusted to your culture that you fit into it without even thinking.

2. **Instead**, fix your attention on God. You'll be changed from the inside out.

3. **Readily recognize** what he wants from you, and **quickly respond** to it.

4. Unlike the culture around you, always **dragging you down** to its level of immaturity, God brings the best out of you, **develops** well-formed maturity in you."

Go and transform your world!

Today's Rhema Word – Week 13, Day 3

HUMBLE YOURSELF AND ASK

To humbly receive wise correction adorns your life with beauty and makes you a better person. (Proverbs 25:11 TPT)

Wise counsel is meant to adorn, like a woman who dresses in the morning and, as a final touch, puts on a beautiful piece of jewelry to finish off her look. She feels good and looks good.

There are times when we get stuck in life, and are uncertain about how to move forward, emotionally, and physically. God has placed people in our lives who know us and love us. If we are humble enough to listen and receive from loved ones their beautiful words of wisdom, we can be unstuck. Movement happens in our life when we listen to and take the advice of those who love us and want something **for us not from us**. The result will always be a life of beauty. It's like the final touches to our life that allow us to walk into our destiny.

If you're ever stuck, ask those around you to speak into your life. Don't wait until everything comes to a complete standstill and you find yourself going nowhere.

**Humble yourself, open your mouth,
and ask for their words of wisdom.**

Learn from Proverbs

Proverbs 12:15 says a fool is _____
but a wise man _____.
Proverbs 19:20 says you can be wise if you _____ and _____.
Proverbs 13:10 says wisdom _____
but pride _____.
Proverbs 1:5 defines a wise man as someone who _____
_____.
Proverbs 15:22 says when you lack counsel your plans _____.

Challenging Us to Live for Jesus

There are times when the wise counsel we receive is advice, opinions, or something we need to know. It can also come through asking good questions, challenging us to think and do new things, and offering comfort to help us heal and grow.

Describe how you have received from either or both ways:
_____
_____

Listen to the Right Counsel, Then Go and Do

Beware: Psalm 1:1 says, do not _____
Instead, follow Psalm 1:2 which says, _____

Today's Rhema Word – Week 13, Day 4

BUILD HIS KINGDOM

"And I also say to you that you are Peter,
*and on this rock **I will build My church**,*
and the gates of Hades shall not prevail against it."
(Matthew 16:18 NKJV)

Jesus never tasked us with building His Church. Jesus tasked us with building His Kingdom. When the Church focuses on the Kingdom, the King will focus on the Church. We are to make ourselves available absolutely anywhere and everywhere we go. We are to share across denominational lines. We are to reach across socio-economic lines. We are to serve across racial and ethnic lines. When fellow believers need our help, we bless them even if they are connected to a different church family.

Father God is about local gatherings of believers, but He's called us to the highways and byways, the least and the lost, the disenfranchised and the downtrodden.

He's calling us to get outside of our boxes. In fact, you can't find God in a box. The only time He's in a box is to come and get us out of ours so we can go and do what He has called us to do. Let's make ourselves available to those He puts in our pathway and watch Him build His Church.

Learn from the Apostle Paul and Jesus

Jesus never tasked us with building His **Church**. Jesus tasked us with building His **Kingdom**.

What is the difference between His Church and His Kingdom?
His Church is (see Ephesians 1:22-23, 1 Corinthians 1:2) _____

_____

God's Kingdom is (see Luke 17:20-21) _____

_____

Live and Love for Jesus

Jesus calls us to make ourselves available anywhere and everywhere we go. He said go into **all** the world.

How are you going to go and do His will in each of these areas?

Share across denominational lines _____

_____

Reach across socio-economic lines _____

_____

Serve across racial and ethnic lines _____

_____

Go to the highways and byways _____

_____

Go to the least and the lost _____

_____

Go to the disenfranchised and the downtrodden

_____

Today's Rhema Word – Week 13, Day 5

SUDDENLIES

"Now it happened, as I journeyed and came near Damascus at about noon, SUDDENLY a great light from heaven shone around me. And I fell to the ground and heard a voice saying to me, 'Saul, Saul, why are you persecuting Me?'"
(Acts 22:6-7 NKJV)

God is an expert at "suddenlies." One moment, Paul was a murderer of the beloved, the next moment a miner of souls for the Kingdom. Never lose sight that at any moment in the midst of your circumstance, a suddenly can happen! Whether you're in a season of hiddenness, a time of waiting for God's promotion, in a place of indecision about what's next, or praying for a breakthrough for yourself or a loved one, know that the God of "suddenlies" can come at any moment. I live in that reality.

We are encouraged in Scripture to do our part, stay the course, and not grow weary in doing good, for in due time we will reap. In the meantime, let's allow God to do His special work in us. No time waiting goes to waste as God works His plan and purpose in our lives.

We, as His sons and daughters, get to enjoy His presence on a daily basis. He is faithful. That's His nature. That's who He is. Be ready for the suddenlies of God in your life!

Learn While in God's Waiting Room

We need to allow God to do His special work in us and realize no time waiting goes to waste. God will send His suddenlies and transform our waiting into fulfillment.

Are you in a season of hiddenness? _____

A time of waiting for God's promotion? _____

A place of indecision about what's next? _____

Praying for a breakthrough for yourself or a loved one?

Use Psalm 27:14 as your declaration as you wait.

I will wait for and confidently expect the LORD to bring His suddenly concerning my situation. I will be strong and let my heart take courage; Yes, I will wait for and confidently expect the LORD's suddenly!

Live for Jesus

God expects you to do your part.

Stay the course for me means I need to

_____

_____

Declare Galatians 6:9. *I will not grow weary of doing good, for in due season, I know I will reap if I do not give up. I want to be ready for when God suddenly directs me to go and do.*

Week 13, Day 6

HEARING & OBEYING GOD'S VOICE

REFLECTION QUESTIONS FOR YOU TO ANSWER THIS WEEK...

This week we explored how God uses our waiting room experiences to get us ready for the "suddenlies" He wants to drop into our lives. Our quote for this week is so on target as our world is rapidly moving into a new, challenging season for us as sons and daughters of God.

1. We were warned about the potential of cultures mixing into Christian ministry and producing "strange fruit" that is not of God. *What does this mean to you personally as you seek to obey His directive to go and transform your world?*

    _____

    _____

2. *Why is it so important for you to listen to the right counsel before you Go and Do what is needed to build His Kingdom?*

    _____

    _____

Remember, God will send His suddenlies and transform your waiting into His wonders.

"Give me 100 preachers who fear nothing but sin
and desire nothing but God;
such alone will shake the gates of hell."

— John Wesley[29]

Today's Rhema Word – Week 14, Day 1

ALL EYES ON HIM

So that no one may boast before him.
(1 Corinthians 1:29 NIV)

I love this simple verse. Think about it for a minute. The Father wants to make it clear that what you are experiencing is Him. When God really moves, it leaves no room for doubt or for anyone else to take credit for His marvelous acts. This is how you know you are beginning to move in the things of the Spirit. When He does stuff that you can't do and everyone else knows you can't do it.

He wants all the attention. He wants all the applause. He wants all eyes on Him. He's the One who can change everything about a human life. We can say thank You to Him for demonstrating His awesome presence and power in our lives, but we must move to the side and let Him do His perfect work. For me, this is a reminder to do a quick heart check.

When He moves, it's powerful, and we must be prepared to be His living vessels to the world. We also must be prepared to step to the side in our hearts so Jesus can do what He does best.

Learn from Jesus

Time to do a quick heart check.

Ask Yourself…

Am I taking credit? _____

Do I live for the applause? _____

Am I asking people what they think of my performance in order to feel better about myself? _____

Remember what Proverbs 23:7 says:

_____

_____

Live Like Jesus

Everything Jesus did gave glory to God the Father.

Read and complete John 15:8 (NIV).

"This is to _____ glory, that you bear much fruit, showing yourselves to be my _____."

Love through Jesus (go and do)

Go and do 2 Corinthians 4:6: "For God, who said, 'Let light shine out of darkness,' made his light shine in our hearts to give us the light of the knowledge of **God's glory** displayed in the face of Christ" (NIV).

Remember 1 Corinthians 10:31 says, "So whether you eat or drink or whatever you do, do it all for the **glory of God**" (NIV).

Today's Rhema Word – Week 14, Day 2

STEWARDS OF THE MYSTERIES OF GOD

*Let a man so consider us as servants of Christ
and stewards of the mysteries of God.*
(1 Corinthians 4:1 NKJV)

This is a verse I discovered while listening to a message about learning to steward the voice of God. God speaks to us and nothing He says is wasteful. It's such a privilege when He communicates with us. Sometimes, He speaks to me, and I don't understand. At that moment, it doesn't make sense, but that's okay. In whatever form He speaks to me, I write it down. I even categorize the ways He speaks to me as dreams, visions, impressions, words, etc.

When we write down all that we hear Him say to us, it lets Him know we care and trust Him. It sends the message that we value every word He speaks. When we do that, He is delighted to speak even more.

Mystery is the lifeblood of intimacy. When He speaks it draws us closer to Him and that's the point. "Listen up...."

Ask Yourself...
What is the Father saying to me?

Literally, His words create worlds (see Genesis 1).

Learn from Apostle James

Why is it so important to watch the words we speak more carefully?

_____

Read James 3:9-10. "With the tongue we _____ our Lord and Father, and with it we _____ human beings, who have been made in _____ likeness. Out of the same mouth come _____ and _____. My brothers and sisters, this should _____ be."

Live Like Jesus

Define a steward: _____

See 1 Corinthians 4:1 in the Amplified Translation. "So then, let us [who minister] be regarded as servants of Christ and stewards (trustees, administrators) of the mysteries of God [that He chooses to reveal]."

What are the responsibilities of a good steward?

_____

How does this apply to the mysteries of God He chooses to reveal to us?

_____

Love through Jesus (go and do)

Mystery is the lifeblood of intimacy. When He speaks it draws us closer to Him and that's the point.

What is the Father saying to you?

Write it down in your journal or phone even if you do not understand it yet. Periodically refer back to it.

Today's Rhema Word – Week 14, Day 3

KNOW MY HEART

Search me, O God, and know my heart; Try me, and know
my anxieties; And see if there is any wicked way in me and
lead me in the way everlasting.
(Psalm 139:23-24 NKJV)

I find that getting closer to Father God is not just about power. You also begin to become aware of areas within us we need Jesus to change or deepen. I've experienced this in the area of selfishness. I consider myself at times selfless. I'm willing to put others first. The closer I get to the Father, the more I realize He wants more. He's calling me to deeper levels of selflessness.

David makes it clear that there is always more. He invites God to search his heart and show him what's needed. Then he said, "try me" which is simply the process of applying pressure to areas of our lives to reveal a deeper need for Jesus. Once those things are revealed, we get to give them to Him. Jesus makes the exchange, giving us something far better, more of Him. It's an amazing yet uncomfortable process of growth, but it's worth it.

David was a man who captured God's heart. I'll take his advice on this one.

Learn from David

In Acts 13:22, God said, "I have found David, son of Jesse, a man after my own heart [because] _____

_____."

What do you want God to say about you? _____

Live Like You're After God's Own Heart

David was called a man after God's own heart because:

      he never made a mistake   he repented

      he covered up his sin   he admitted his sin

      he had faith in God   he was a good leader

Read what David said in Psalm 51.

What does this show about David's heart?

_____

_____

Love through Jesus (go and do)

David invited God to search his heart and show him what was needed. Jesus makes the exchange, giving you something far better.

Will you do the same? _____

What changes is Jesus asking you to make?

_____

_____

Today's Rhema Word – Week 14, Day 4

FAITHFUL IN THE LEAST OF THESE

He who is faithful in what is least is faithful also in much;
and he who is unjust in what is least is unjust also in much.
Therefore if you have not been faithful in the unrighteous mammon,
who will commit to your trust the true riches?
And if you have not been faithful in what is another man's,
who will give you what is your own?
(Luke 16:10-12 NKJV)

Stewardship is huge in the Kingdom. God is looking to see how we are taking care of the simple things in our lives, like finances, cleaning up behind ourselves, contributing to our households, and how we use our time, gifts, and talents.

Before God trusts us with the supernatural,
He watches how we steward things in the natural.

There is a direct link between these seemingly insignificant things and the Kingdom ministry our Father wants to assign to us. Let's pay attention to the simple things around us in the natural and steward them well.

Then, hold on and watch how Jesus will begin to give us Kingdom assignments that touch the lives of those around us.

Learn from Jesus

Read the Parable of the Talents in Matthew 25:14-30.

Verse 21 says, "His lord said to him, 'Well done, good and faithful servant; you were faithful over a few things, I will make you _____.

Enter into the _____."'

What insight did the Holy Spirit reveal to you from the parable?

_____

Live Like Jesus

Pay attention to the simple things around you in the natural and steward them well.

What does God see when He looks at how you are taking care of the simple things in your life like finances, cleaning up behind yourself, contributing to your household, and how you use your time, gifts, and talents?

_____

What changes do you need to make to have God move you into the Kingdom ministry God wants to assign for you?

_____

_____

Love through Jesus (go and do)

How has Jesus begun to give you Kingdom assignments that touch the lives of those around you?

_____

_____

Today's Rhema Word – Week 14, Day 5

HIS SHEKINAH GLORY

And He said, "My Presence will go with you, and I will give you rest."
(Exodus 33:14 NKJV)

W*hy do we gather together?* We might conclude several reasons: to worship, serve, hear the Word of the Lord, and give our tithes and offerings. These are correct, but there is a central purpose as to why we gather on Sunday or Wednesday evening or for special services. We gather to meet Him and to be in the manifest presence of Almighty God. It's what the Hebrews refer to as the *Shekinah* and the *Kavod* manifestation of the presence of God.

What happens when God does show up?

Will we continue with the gathering, business as usual?

Will we rush on to the next thing in the order of the service?

Will we scurry out the door so we can watch our favorite sporting event?

We love the Word of God, but will we send His presence away just so we can get to the message?

His presence is a gift. We must be sensitive to when He enters the room and allow the Holy Spirit to dictate to the leadership what's next.

**When His presence comes,
you will never be the same.**

Learn from Jesus

What happens when His Shekinah glory shows up?

In Exodus 13:20-22, it _____

In Exodus 33:9, God told Moses, _____

How is it described in 2 Corinthians 3:18? _____

Live Like Jesus

Shekinah glory is experienced in your life when you take the time to lean into and allow the Holy Spirit to work in your life.

**When His presence comes,
you will never be the same.**

Have you experienced His shekinah glory in your life? _____

Explain: _____

Love through Jesus (go and do)

In Matthew 27:51, what happened when the shekinah glory fell upon the temple? _____

What was happening at the time that caused this to happen?

_____

How did this change the world forever? _____

Week 14, Day 6

HEARING & OBEYING GOD'S VOICE

REFLECTION QUESTIONS FOR YOU TO ANSWER THIS WEEK...

This week we learned there is a direct link between these seemingly insignificant things and the Kingdom ministry our Father wants to assign to us.

1. However, we learned that before God trusts us with the supernatural, He watches how we steward even the insignificant things in the natural.

How has this powerful truth changed the way you steward the life God has already given you?

_____

_____

_____

2. *Do I want to shake the gates of hell and fulfill my mission powerfully through God's presence in my life?* _____

How does my life prove I fear nothing but sin and desire nothing but God, so I am ready for His assignment?

_____

_____

_____

"Grace does not cancel out our
responsibility or accountability
for the things God has given us to do."
— Mike Bickle[30]

Today's Rhema Word – Week 15, Day 1

SET APART

You are to be holy to me because I, the LORD, am holy,
and I have set you apart from the nations to be my own.
(Leviticus 20:26 NIV)

God has established Himself as Holy. He is pure and perfect. He is above all other gods. He sits high and lifted up. Every created thing and every human being on earth bows before Him. What's interesting is that He calls us to be like Him. HOLY!

How can we become Holy?

It doesn't have anything to do with perfection or following any type of rules. God defines it in the last sentence of Leviticus 20:26. **He has set us apart.** That means we have a specific purpose and use in His Kingdom on this earth. It means He has created us for Himself and not for anyone or any other use.

In the natural, every invention has an intended use. If that use is not understood, it will be misused or abused. When we forget or do not understand our Kingdom use, we open ourselves up to be misused or even abused.

Let's set ourselves apart daily for God's perfect use.

Learn from Jesus

What does it mean to be chosen and set apart by God?

How are we to act and think that shows the world we are the set apart of God and ambassadors of Christ?

Read 1 Peter 2:9-11 to find your answers.

_____

_____

Live Like Jesus

In the natural, every invention has an intended use. If that is not understood, it will be misused or abused.

Have you found you have forgotten or not understood your Kingdom use and been misused and even abused? _____

Why has God set you apart in His Kingdom?

_____

_____

Love through Jesus (go and do)

1Peter 1:13 (NIV) tells you how you can go and do your true, "set-apart," Kingdom purpose:

prepare your _____ for action

be _____

set your hope _____ on _____

Verse 14 adds: do not _____ to _____

Verse 17 says, live your lives as _____

Today's Rhema Word – Week 15, Day 2

YOUR "GOD" DESIGN

For every word God speaks is sure and every promise pure.
His truth is tested, found to be flawless, and ever faithful.
It's as pure as silver refined seven times in a crucible of clay.
(Psalm 12:6 TPT)

What has God spoken over you through His Word, prophecy, sermon, or any other means?

_____

_____

Hold on to His Word. It is dependable. You can count on it to come true. In fact, His Word begins the process of leading you into your "God" design. Don't worry about your current circumstances, they don't carry any weight. They literally are irrelevant. What's important is what God is saying over you. Stay focused! Stay hungry!

God's Word accomplishes His purpose.

God is dependable and faithful to His Word.

God keeps His word even if men don't.

His Word will come to pass no matter what

people do, say, or believe.

God's Word will work for you
if you will believe it!

Learn How God's Word Will Work for You

God is dependable and faithful to His Word.

Proverbs 30:5 says, "Every word of God proves _____; he is a _____ to those who take refuge in him" (ESV).

God keeps His word even if men don't.

Numbers 23:19 says, "God is not man, that he should _____, or a son of man, that he should _____ his _____." (ESV)

No matter what people do, say, or believe, His Word accomplishes His purpose.

Isaiah 55:11 says, "So shall my _____ be that goes out from my mouth; it shall not return to me _____, but it shall _____ that which I _____, and shall _____ in the thing for which I sent it" (ESV).

His Word is beginning the process of leading you into your "God" design.

What have you discovered is your "God" design?

_____

Remember, your current circumstances don't carry any weight.

Stay Focused! Never...never give up.

Today's Rhema Word – Week 15, Day 3

HUMBLE OR HUMILIATED

And lest I should be exalted above measure by the abundance of the revelations, a thorn in the flesh was given to me, a messenger of Satan to buffet me, lest I be exalted above measure.
(2 Corinthians 12:7 NKJV)

No one knows what the thorn was that afflicted Paul. What we do know is why it was allowed in his life. It had to do with divine revelation from God. Something happens to us as we become more and more aware of the spiritual realm. I don't believe the greater the revelation we receive the greater the thorn to afflict. I believe Paul is sharing the great need for humility. It's easy to get prideful when God uses us in miraculous ways. It feels amazing. Even when we want to be humble, many will try and exalt us and make us into their objects of worship. Beware!

Great humility is necessary for great revelation.

We see in Luke 14:11 where Jesus says we have a choice. We can humble ourselves, or we can be humiliated, which means someone else humbles us.

Let's pursue a life of humility as we seek greater revelation from the Father.

Warnings from James and Jesus

Read the warning in James 4:10.

What does it mean to exalt yourself? _____

What happens if you do? _____

What did Jesus say in Matthew 23:12?

_____

_____

Warnings from Paul and Barnabas

What happened when Paul and Barnabas were used mightily by God in Acts 14:11-13?

_____

_____

How did Paul and Barnabas respond in Acts 14:14-18?

_____

_____

Learn from Others Then Go and Do

We need to pursue a life of humility as we seek greater revelation from the Father.

Research other biblical and modern-day examples of Christian leaders who pursued a life of humility and were used by God to bring revelation to the people of God. For example: John the Baptist, Ruth, Mother Teresa, Morris Cerullo, and Billy Graham.

What did you learn from studying these people?

_____

Today's Rhema Word – Week 15, Day 4

ALONE TIME WITH JESUS

The council members were astonished as they witnessed the bold courage of Peter and John, especially when they discovered that they were just ordinary men who had never had religious training. Then they began to understand the effect Jesus had on them simply by spending time with him. (Acts 4:13 TPT emphasis added)

John and Peter were two of Jesus' disciples. They weren't church professionals, but they were set apart as different. They were bold and courageous. They prayed for people and miracles happened. The religious leaders of their time took notice and realized these guys had spent time with Jesus.

It's not how much time we spend at church that gives us power from on high. It's the time we spend with Jesus. It's the amount of time we allow ourselves to become "the church" when we're in the community, school, and marketplace. This is what sets us apart and calls the attention of others.

Find your alone time with Jesus, go for long walks, and have an open conversation with Him. Read the Bible asking the Holy Spirit to teach you about His nature and His ways. Fast and pray asking God for Ephesians 1:17-19. If you do some of these things, you will experience a remarkable difference in your relationship with Jesus, and others will know and benefit from Who you hang out with.

Alone Time with Jesus

What are you asking God to do when you pray for Ephesians 1:17-19 in your life?

_____

_____

_____

_____

Live Like Jesus

What have others noticed about your life now that you spend more alone time with Jesus?

Friends or neighbors _____

_____

People at school or work _____

_____

Others _____

Love through Jesus (go and do)

How has your ministry to others been affected by spending more alone time with Jesus?

_____

_____

_____

IRREVOCABLE

For the gifts and the calling of God are irrevocable.
(Romans 11:29 NKJV)

God doesn't take His gifts and calling back! If I were to be honest, I've been in seasons where I wanted to give back to God His calling on my life. Perhaps, I felt unworthy, underserving, too sinful, or unqualified. He responded to me, "Since when has it ever been about you?" That's right! It's not about me or you. It never was and never will be. It's always been about Him and His master plan. He knows exactly what He wants to accomplish with you and me. He's given us specific callings and set within us gifts to get it done. They NEVER go away. We can sit on them and not use them, but they are still there. They are a part of our spiritual DNA.

Even if we decide not to use our gifts and step into our calling, He still holds us accountable. We still will see Him face-to-face and give an account of what we did or did not do with what He has given us. Once I realized this fact, I fell to my knees and thanked God for His calling and gifts. Now, I eagerly serve Him in whatever capacity is in front of me.

Dial into your calling and gifts.
Start where you are and do what's in front of you for His glory.
Your Spiritual DNA

Irrevocable means: (circle correct definitions)

final	beyond recall	revokable	alterable
changeable	returnable	irreversible	
permanent	flexible	conclusive	

Live Like Jesus

It's not about you or me! That's an eye-opener as we seek to live like Jesus. Complete what Jesus said in John 15:16.

"You did _____ choose Me, but I _____ you and _____ you that you should go and bear fruit, and *that* your fruit should _____, that whatever you ask the Father in My name He may give you" (NKJV).

How does this change the way you look at the gifts and the calling of God on your life?

_____

_____

Love through Jesus (go and do)

Thank God for His calling and gifts.
   Eagerly serve Him in whatever capacity is in front of you.
      Dial into your calling and gifts.
         Start where you are and do what's in front of you for His glory.

**He is holding you accountable
for what He has given you.**

Week 15, Day 6

HEARING & OBEYING GOD'S VOICE

REFLECTION QUESTIONS FOR YOU TO ANSWER THIS WEEK...

This week we learned God holds us accountable for all that He has given us even if we chose not to use the gifts or walk in His calling.

For the gifts and the calling of God are irrevocable.
(Romans 11:29 NKJV)

**He is holding you accountable
for what He has given you.**

1. We are accountable for how we live our everyday lives. Romans 14:12 says, "So then, each of us will give an account of ourselves to God" (NKJV).

How has this amazing revelation changed your day-to-day life and choices?

_____

_____

2. When we forget or do not understand our Kingdom calling, we open ourselves up to be misused or even abused.

Write down how you now are more aware of your Kingdom calling and how God wants you to use it to fulfill His mission for you?

_____

_____

"Though we are incomplete, God loves us completely. Though we are imperfect, He loves us perfectly. Though we may feel lost and without a compass, God's love encompasses us completely. ...
He loves every one of us, even those who are flawed, rejected, awkward, sorrowful, or broken."

—Dieter F. Uchtdorf[31]

Today's Rhema Word – Week 16, Day 1

BEHIND THE VEIL

This hope we have as an anchor of the soul, both sure and steadfast, and which enters the Presence behind the veil. (Hebrews 6:19 NKJV)

There was a thick curtain in the Jewish temple that separated the Holy of Holies from the rest of the temple. It's where the high priest would go once a year to bring a sacrifice before God for the sins of the nation.

The Bible says the moment Jesus died on the cross, the veil in the temple was torn down the middle from the top to the bottom. God was saying, "Now ALL who are called sons and daughters have **full** access to Me. Come behind the veil and know Me." Your invitation today is to come behind the veil and know the Father.

When you spend time behind the veil, everyone will know it. Your countenance, your speech, and how you live and love will change. You'll walk in power. His fruit will begin to spring up in your life. In fact, you'll see His fruit spring up in the lives of those you go around and influence.

If you come looking for us, you'll find us behind the veil. Will you join us?

Will You Accept the Invitation?

Jesus paid the price for your invitation.

What does it say in the Parable of the Wedding Feast if someone refuses to accept God's invitation? (See Matthew 22:1-14)

_____

_____

Live Like a Disciple of Jesus

What did Jesus tell His disciples in Mark 6:7-12 when He sent them out two by two?

_____

_____

Love through Jesus (go and do)

What is the primary message of the four Gospels?

_____

_____

_____

Why are they referred to as the "Good News"?

_____

_____

Why is this so relevant in today's world?

_____

_____

_____

Today's Rhema Word – Week 16, Day 2

ENDLESS, EXTRAVAGANT LOVE

Then you will be empowered to discover what every holy one expe-
riences—the great magnitude of the astonishing love of Christ in all
its dimensions. How deeply intimate and far-reaching is his love!
How enduring and inclusive it is! Endless love beyond measurement
that transcends our understanding—this extravagant love pours
into you until you are filled to overflowing with the fullness of God!
(Ephesians 3:19 TPT)

It's important to pause and think for a moment about how deeply we are known and loved by God, our eternal Father. We can spend a lifetime in the shadows of regret and guilt if not for the purifying and cleansing love of our Heavenly Father.

His love is so pure it strips us of anything that keeps us from becoming who He created us to become. His love carries our identity and calls us into His purpose. His love calls us away from self-loathing to self-loving.

As we accept His love for ourselves, sonship is fully in place. Now we have the power to love those around us and call them into their purpose and destiny in Christ.

Let Father God love you today, then rise up and be His love to someone else who needs it desperately.

Learn to Move Out of the Shadows

You can spend a lifetime in the shadows of regret and guilt if not for the purifying and cleansing love of your Heavenly Father that calls you away from self-loathing to self-loving.

Read, memorize, and declare 1 John 1:7 and 9 over your life.

_____

_____

_____

Live Like Jesus

What does Romans 8:1 tell you? _____

Read and receive Romans 8:15-17.

As you accept His love, your sonship is fully in place. Now you have the power to love those around you and call them into their purpose and destiny in Christ.

Love through Jesus (go and do)

What does Ephesians 5:1-2 say is your assignment?

_____

_____

Let Father God's endless, extravagant love fill you today, then rise up and be His love to someone else who needs it desperately.

Today's Rhema Word – Week 16, Day 3

YOUR AUTHENTIC DESIGN

And he who had died came out bound hand and foot with graveclothes,
and his face was wrapped with a cloth. Jesus said to them,
"Loose him, and let him go."
(John 11:44 NKJV)

What are graveclothes? They are anything that keeps us from being our authentic design. There is a unique design God has put in us. It's the very reason He created us and called us to Himself as sons and daughters. Remember: God is not just the Alpha (first Greek letter of the alphabet), He is also the Omega (last Greek letter of the alphabet). He is at the end, and He sees your full potential realized. He's calling you into it now.

Graveclothes bind you and stop you from becoming who you are called to be. They attempt to form you into someone or something that is not you. When that happens, we begin to go through the motions of life. The Apostle Paul says having a "form but lacking the power within." The power of God descends on us when we find who He created us to be.

There is freedom and joy when the graveclothes come off and you stand before Jesus and say, "Here I am, Lord, send me." Shed the graveclothes and partner with Holy Spirit to become who He created you to be.

Reveal Your Authentic Design

Read Galatians 5:1, 5:13.

Ask Yourself…

Do I know who I really am? _____

What are the passions in my heart?

_____

_____

What burdens are stopping me from becoming all my Heavenly Father has designed me to become?

_____

_____

Live Like Jesus

Jesus said to them, "Loose him, and let him go." (John 11:44)

Ephesians 2:1-2a says, "As for you, you were _____ in your transgressions and _____, in which you used to _____ when you followed the ways of this _____" (NIV). Go to your trusted prayer partner or good friend and ask him or her to do what Jesus told His disciples to do for Lazarus. Then partner together with the Holy Spirit so you can go and be who God has called you to be for Him.

Love through Jesus (go and do)

Now, stand before Jesus and say aloud, "Here I am, Lord, send me."

I hope you're ready for Him to respond!

Today's Rhema Word – Week 16, Day 4

LISTEN FOR THE VOICE OF GOD

Whether you turn to the right or to the left,
your ears will hear a voice behind you,
saying, "This is the way; walk in it."
(Isaiah 30:21 NIV)

The voice of God literally guides our lives. Isaiah is reassuring us there is no place we can go where we can hide from the voice of God.

As His son or daughter, you are followed by the voice of God like a flashlight in the darkness. Inherent in His voice is your destiny. His powerful voice created worlds. He knows the end from the beginning. His voice also sets in place the guardrails for your life.

As a son or daughter, why wouldn't you seek to listen to your Heavenly Father's voice?

Listen for His voice.

Listen carefully to what He is saying to you.

Don't question His voice. OBEY!

Surround yourself with mature believers who can help you interpret His voice.

Get ready for the best journey of your life.

Learn to Listen for the Voice of God

Isaiah 30:21says your ears will hear a _____.

1 Kings 19:11-13 says God's voice sounds like

_____

_____

In Jeremiah 23:29, God said His words were like _____

_____

What did Jesus say about hearing what God says in John 8:47?

_____

Listen so You Can Live Like Jesus

Surround yourself with mature believers who can help you interpret His voice.

Who have you surrounded yourself with to receive the counsel you need to interpret God's voice?

_____

_____

Listen so You can Love, Go, and Do

Listen carefully to what He is saying to you.
    Don't question His voice. OBEY!
        Get ready for the best journey of your life.

What has God instructed you to go and do?

_____

_____

Today's Rhema Word – Week 16, Day 5

EXPRESSIONS

Until then (seeing God face to face), there are three things that remain: faith, hope, and love—yet love surpasses them all. So above all else, let love be the beautiful prize for which you run.
(1 Corinthians 13:13 TPT)

The word the Holy Spirit is bringing to my mind is "Expressions." Paul is speaking in the context of spiritual gifts. He's basically saying once we get to Heaven, spiritual gifts will drop off in significance., but what will remain with us until then are faith, hope, and love, especially love.

Paul was showing us that love is a spiritual reality of a different kind. We read about it in the scriptures, so we know it's true. We have felt it from time to time, but have we ever paused long enough to realize that love is God's secret sauce? It's a sauce that has so many ingredients and so many uses or expressions that I think we miss it sometimes. Even in negative circumstances, His love is present.

Our entire journey as followers of Jesus is about His love toward us, in us, and through us. Take the time today to become more aware of His expressions of love. Look everywhere you go today.

Love exists because He does.

Learn to Look for Expressions of His Love

1 John 4:12 says God's love is expressed:

_____

_____

Romans 8:37-39 says God's love is expressed:

_____

_____

Learn to Express Love Like Jesus

In Matthew 9:12-13, read what Jesus told the Pharisees who were criticizing Him for having dinner with tax collectors and sinners.

How was Jesus expressing the love of God the Father?

_____

_____

Go and Express God's Love

Become living examples of God's love.

- ♥ Share kind words
- ♥ Encourage and build up others
- ♥ Give hope
- ♥ Bring joy and comfort
- ♥ Pray for others
- ♥ Spend time and resources with others
- ♥ Other examples:

_____

_____

Week 16, Day 6

HEARING & OBEYING GOD'S VOICE

REFLECTION QUESTIONS FOR YOU TO ANSWER THIS WEEK...

This week you learned that spending time behind the veil will change your countenance, your speech, and how you live and love. You'll walk in power, and His fruit will begin to spring up in your life. In fact, you'll see His fruit spring up in the lives of those you go around and influence.

1. *How has this manifested in your life now that you understand the power of spending time behind the Veil?*

   _____

   _____

   _____

   _____

2. Your entire journey as a follower of Jesus is about His love toward you, in you, and through you.

How has His amazing, extravagant, and endless love changed your life, and how your life impacts others?

   _____

   _____

   _____

   _____

"All of God's people are ordinary people
who have been made extraordinary
by the purpose he has given them."

— Oswald Chambers[32]

Today's Rhema Word – Week 17, Day 1

BY MY SPIRIT

So he answered and said to me: "This is the word of the LORD to Zerubbabel: 'Not by might nor by power, but by My Spirit,' Says the LORD of hosts.
(Zechariah 4:6 NKJV)

Look around at the condition of our world and ask yourself…

As I look at the world and see the chaos, the violence, the impact of the global pandemic, racial tension, and the poor choices and decisions our political leaders are making, does it fill me with a sense of helplessness?

What does it look like when I am at the end of my human strength?

What does it feel like not to have the answers to the hard questions I'm being asked?

What does it feel like to see the suffering around me and not have the solutions to the difficult human dilemmas?

I personally feel powerless. Here's a prayer I pray, maybe more than any other, "Father, keep me humble, let me feel what You feel for people, and give me the power and the wisdom to do something about it." Join me in that prayer.

Learn From the Lord of Hosts

"Not by might nor by power, but by My Spirit," says the Lord of hosts. These words were not spoken just for the prophets of old. They are just as relevant in our lives today. It seems even as Christians, we have become complacent and feel it is someone else's job to fix or change what is wrong in our world.

Ask yourself, who is responsible for fixing the chaos and human dilemmas I see all around me?

scientists   politicians   doctors

military advisors   world leaders   the wealthy

Christian leaders   local leaders

What is my personal responsibility?

_____

_____

Seek God's Spirit

How do I personally tap into what the Lord is telling me will bring the changes needed in our world?

It begins with individual prayer and should include corporate prayer as well. God's Spirit is the only one who can lead us in the right direction.

Romans 8:26 says, "In the same way, the _____ helps us in our weakness. We do not know what we ought to pray for, but the _____ himself _____ for us through wordless groans" (NIV).

Today's Rhema Word – Week 17, Day 2

JOB WAS A WINNER

And the LORD restored Job's losses when he prayed for his friends.
Indeed the LORD gave Job twice as much as he had before.
(Job 42:10 NKJV)

Jesus said that anyone who gives up something for the Kingdom of God will be repaid (Luke 18:29-30). Our restoration may or may not be the same kind as Job's, which was both spiritual and material. Interestingly, Job's restoration was also tied to his ability to pray for his friends. If you remember, his friends had turned their backs on Job. God's blessings turn to us when we forgive. Forgiveness is the pathway to freedom.

Job won his spiritual life with God, doubled all his material possessions, and won back his friendships and family. Job was a winner!

Our complete restoration will happen. God loves us, and He is just. He will not only restore whatever we have lost; He will give us more than we can imagine.

Cling tightly to Jesus through all your trials, and you, too, will be rewarded by the Father.

Learn From Job

Satan's accusation of Job was

_____

_____

What was God's reply to Satan? _____

Job's three friends accused him of

_____

_____

_____

How did Job reply to his friend's accusations?

_____

_____

What did Job accuse God of? _____

What was God's reply to Job?

_____

_____

Forgive Like Job

What did God tell Job he needed to do? _____

_____

What was Job's restoration tied to? _____

What was Job's reward from God? _____

_____

Cling tightly to Jesus through all your trials and forgive those who accuse you when you have done nothing wrong, and you, too, will be rewarded by the Father.

Today's Rhema Word – Week 17, Day 3

GOD IS CALLING YOUR NAME

*And they heard the sound of the LORD God walking in the garden
in the cool of the day, and Adam and his wife hid themselves from
the presence of the LORD God among the trees of the garden.*
(Genesis 3:8 NKJV)

Adam and his wife Eve had just partnered with the devil (the ser-
pent) inviting sin into the world and initiating what is called "the
Fall." Their eyes were immediately opened, and they became aware of
their sinfulness and disobedience toward God. It was man who hid
from God, not God who hid from man. God, being all-knowing, knew
they had sinned, right? That means God's first response to original sin
was an act of intimacy and relationship.

When we sin, our first response is to hide from ourselves (that's
called denial), and then we hide our sin from others. By doing those
two things, we're attempting to hide from God. God's solution to sin is
to come and find us. He's not angry. His solution to sin is found in the
context of intimacy and relationship.

First, honesty with yourself, then honesty with others. This is when
you get to experience the love of your Father. God still walks in the cool
of His garden calling your name. Let's always respond.

Learn From Apostle James

Instead of attempting to hide our sin, James 5:16 says, "Therefore, confess (*share*) your sins to one another [your false steps, your offenses], and pray for one another, that you may be healed *and* restored. The heartfelt *and* persistent prayer of a righteous man (believer) can accomplish much [when put into action and made effective by God— it is dynamic and can have tremendous power]" (AMP).

Underline or highlight the powerful truths James revealed in this passage that will help you more effectively deal with sin and the struggles in your life.

Honesty Is the Answer

How will honesty with yourself and with your trusted prayer partners and friends bring you back into a right relationship with God?

_____

_____

Stop Hiding Among the Trees (Go and Do)

You cannot complete your God-given assignment if you are trying to hide among the trees from God, yourself, and others. God is calling your name!

Today's Rhema Word – Week 17, Day 4

THE ECONOMY OF GOD

"Throughout history there was never found a man as great as John the Baptizer. Yet those who now walk in God's kingdom realm, though they appear to be insignificant, will become even greater than he."
(Jesus in Luke 7:28 TPT)

Here is a perfect example of what I call God's Kingdom Economy. In case you don't know, it was the prophet John the Baptizer who ushered in the ministry of Jesus. He was a forerunner, a foreshadow of what was to come. He led many to look upward to the Father. He ranks high along with others like Moses and Elijah.

In Luke 7:28, Jesus gives us a peek into the economy of God. Some have called it the "upside-down" Kingdom because it is the opposite of how our world functions. He says the least, the insignificant, the weak, the forgotten, the obscure, and the ones in the middle of "nowhere land" are the ones the Father has His eye on. There is so much more the Holy Spirit wants to do in these last days through people like us.

He wants to take ordinary people like us and give us extraordinary purpose and power. We need to expect the greater. I'm looking for it, leaning into it, and available to it. *How about you?*

Learn From Jesus

Jesus gives more insight to this principle as He calls His disciples from among the common folk and outcasts. Look up the names of His disciples and list what they were doing before Jesus called them and what they accomplished in God's Kingdom Economy.

1._____ 2. _____

3. _____ 4. _____

5. _____ 6. _____

7. _____ 8. _____

9. _____ 10. _____

11. _____ 12. _____

Women Used in God's Kingdom Economy

Miriam the Sister_____

Deborah the Judge_____

Esther the Queen_____

Mary the Mother of Jesus_____

Anna the Widow_____

Pricilla the Teacher_____

Lydia the Entrepreneur_____

Lois the Grandmother_____

Mary the Mother of Mark _____

Samaritan Woman at the Well _____

Lazarus' Sister Mary _____

Today's Rhema Word – Week 17, Day 5

YOUR EMMAUS ROAD EXPERIENCE

Then their eyes were opened and they recognized him, and he disappeared from their sight. They asked each other, "Were not our hearts burning within us while he talked with us on the road and opened the Scriptures to us?" (Luke 24:31-32 NIV)

Two of Jesus' disciples had heard the rumors that Jesus' body had been stolen. The promise and prophecy that Jesus would rise on the third day seemed to be empty. In despair and sorrow, they left Jerusalem and headed to a city far away.

Then, something amazing happened. Jesus appeared to them as they were walking away, but they didn't recognize Him. When the disciples finally did recognize Him, Scripture says their hearts burned within them. They were set on fire with passion for Jesus. They quickly headed back to Jerusalem to continue in their calling.

Jesus is calling our attention away from where we are in our journey to look at Him. Do it and let your heart burn from within you. Your promise is alive because Jesus is alive.

Quickly get ready to continue in your calling.

Learn From Jesus

What promises of Jesus have been spoken over your life?

_____

_____

What circumstances have stalled you from moving into that promise?

_____

_____

Your Emmaus Road Experience

Is Jesus trying to get your attention? _____

What has caused you not to recognize Him?

_____

_____

Is He calling you to look away from where you are currently in your life and look to Him? _____

Where do you see Him at work around you? _____

Are you ready for your Emmaus Road experience? _____

Love through Jesus (go and do)

Is your heart burning within you? _____

Declare: My promise is alive because Jesus is alive!

Quickly get ready to go and continue in your calling.

Week 17, Day 6

HEARING & OBEYING GOD'S VOICE

REFLECTION QUESTIONS FOR YOU TO ANSWER THIS WEEK...

This week, you read that it is "Not by might nor by power, but by My Spirit," says the Lord of hosts, and how God is calling your name as He pursues you. God wants to take ordinary people like us and give us extraordinary purpose and power.

1. *What did you learn your extraordinary purpose is in God?*

   _____

   _____

2. *How have this week's lessons impacted your ability to fulfill your God-given purpose?*

   _____

   _____

   _____

   _____

"Of all the glorious things that the blood means,
this is one of the most glorious.
His blood is the sign, the measure yes,
the impartation of His love."

— Andrew Murray[33]

Today's Rhema Word – Week 18, Day 1

THE SHED BLOOD OF JESUS

In the same way, after the supper he took the cup, saying,
"This cup is the new covenant in my blood,
which is poured out for you." (Luke 22:20 NIV)

Jesus shared a meal with His disciples moments before He would face death on a cross. He took a cup full of watered-down wine, held it up, and referenced the New Covenant He was inaugurating. This new covenant was to be made available to all who desired to be a part of it. There would be a new freedom to know and follow God.

To seal the covenant and make it official, blood would have to be shed. The Jewish people would kill an animal, like a lamb, and use its blood to ceremonially seal the deal. In this case, the deal couldn't be sealed by the blood of an animal. It would be sealed by the blood of Jesus. Every drop of blood that came out of His body had an intended person in mind. There is power in His blood. I have determined to never waste one drop of His blood to the best of my ability. His blood is not magic, but it is full of promise and power. However, we must do our part.

Let's not waste one drop of the shed blood of Jesus.
His sacrifice was not in vain.

Learn About the Shed Blood of Jesus

His blood is full of promise and power.
Ephesians 1:7 says we have been _____
Hebrews 10:19 says we have fellowship _____
Isaiah 53:5 says by His stripes we have _____
Revelation 12:11 says we have authority _____
Am I appropriating His blood over my life? _____
Am I maximizing the blood of Jesus personally? _____

Live Like Jesus

Live in the fullness of what Jesus did for you by doing your part.

In Revelation 12:11, *what does it say are the two parts that give you the ability to overcome the attacks of the Devil?*

_____

_____

Love through Jesus (go and do)

This New Covenant is available to all who desire to receive the freedom to know and follow God.

Read Jesus' instructions in Mark 16:15-20.

Now go and share the Good News of this New Covenant, along with your testimony, with everyone the Holy Spirit leads you to.

Today's Rhema Word – Week 18, Day 2

GOD'S NON-PERFORMANCE BASED LOVE

We love Him because He first loved us.
(1 John 4:19 NKJV)

I have lived a great part of my adult life seeking the approval of others, particularly those in authority over me. It goes back to my childhood and my relationship with my father. I learned early I was living in a performance-based love system. The more I achieved, the more I felt loved. There were times in raising my own children that my love was based on how well they performed. I never meant to be that way. It was like a default. It was an honest attempt at helping them be the best at whatever they did.

I'm so blessed we all now have a real and personal relationship with God through Jesus. We have learned He isn't concerned about how well we do things. All He wants is a relationship with each of us. There is something pure and freeing about knowing that.

God loves us for who we are, not for what we can or cannot do. Now I get the awesome privilege of loving my children with the freeing, non-performance love of Jesus. I can sit back and bless their lives as they pursue a love relationship with Jesus.

Learn From God

God loved us first to teach us how to love Him, ourselves, and others.

Read what Jesus said in Matthew 22:37-39.

First, we are to love _____ with all our _____, _____, and _____.

Second, we are to _____ ourselves because the

third step is we are to love our _____ as we love _____.

Love Like Jesus

How did Jesus describe love in John 15:12-13?

_____

_____

_____

God's Non-Performance Based Clause

God's ultimate non-performance-based clause is found in Ephesians 2:8-10.

What amazing truths did you discover in these verses about God's love for you?

_____

_____

_____

Today's Rhema Word – Week 18, Day 3

PERFECT LOVE CASTS OUT FEAR

There is no fear in love; but perfect love casts out fear,
because fear involves torment. But he who fears
has not been made perfect in love.
(1 John 4:18 NKJV)

F ear is a real thing.
Fear is the enemy's number one weapon against God's beloved.
Fear is a spirit sent to undermine our ability to relate to God and man.
Fear is the opposite of faith.
Fear breaks our connection with God.
Fear introduces doubt into the equation causing us to question in our hearts if God is good.
Fear torments our souls and blocks our ability to truly love others.
If fear ever grips your heart, the only solution is perfect love. Perfect love can only come from God. It sends fear running and invites freedom into our souls. Faith returns and what once was a fog over our lives turns into Son-shine.
Let His light shine on you today and be filled with His love.

Dig Deeper and Learn More

Read 1 John 4:18 in the Amplified Translation.

> *There is no fear in love [**dread does not exist**]. But perfect (complete, full-grown) love drives out fear, because fear involves [the expectation of divine] punishment, so the one who is afraid [of God's judgment] is not perfected in love [**has not grown into a sufficient understanding of God's love**].*

Grab ahold of this added insight! Read other translations for even more insight.

Live Like Jesus

Get rid of the "what ifs." That's an enemy tactic that begins as thoughts and then moves into emotions and sometimes leads to poor choices, foolish actions, or an unwillingness to move forward in God's plan.

Proverbs 23:7 says, _____

List your top 3 "what ifs" and defeat them right now by declaring that God loves you and that He is in control. Then cross them off one-by-one!

_____

_____

_____

Let His light shine on you today and be filled with His love, not the enemy's attacks of fear.

Today's Rhema Word – Week 18, Day 4

FIND THE NARROW GATE

"Enter by the narrow gate; for wide is the gate and broad is the way that leads to destruction, and there are many who go in by it.
Because narrow is the gate and difficult is the way which leads to life, and there are few who find it."
(Matthew 7:13-14 NKJV)

Are you looking at the problems and challenges in your life or at what God says about them? The facts are that there are difficulties all around that are ready to define and shape your life. It's not that you want to deny the facts, but you want to allow God's truth to have the final say.

Truth is what God says about you and your circumstance. Often His truth looks radically different than what you are living or experiencing.

So, what do you do? You stay on the narrow road of belief. It's narrow for a reason. Only a few can cling to the truth without giving way to their circumstances. The wide road is well-traveled. It's wide for a reason. It's easier to give in to your circumstance. It's easier to allow the facts to dictate how you live. That's what the majority do, but you are sons and daughters of the Most High God.

Choose the narrow way!

Learn From God's Truth

Are you looking at the problems and challenges in your life or at what God says about them (explain)? _____

God's truth often looks radically different than what you are living or experiencing.

What does God say about you and your circumstance?

_____

_____

Live in God's Truth

Declare I will…

- ➤ stay on the narrow road of belief.
- ➤ always give God's truth the last word.
- ➤ wait upon the Lord when the facts remain, and my circumstance isn't changing until the facts bow to the truth.
- ➤ choose the narrow way!

Show Others the Narrow Way

Because narrow is the gate and difficult is the way which leads to life, and there are few who find it.

As you live your life seeking to stay on the narrow path, encourage others to discover God's truth.

Today's Rhema Word – Week 18, Day 5

PRAY AND SEEK HIS FACE

*"If My people who are called by My name will humble themselves, and pray and seek My face, and turn from their wicked ways, then I will hear from heaven, and will forgive their sin and **heal their land**.*
(2 Chronicles 7:14 NKJV)

Here is the recipe for God's healing:

1. **Humble Yourself**. Acknowledge all is not well. God already knows, but He needs us to admit it. Lay aside pride. Then pray, "HELP!" That's a prayer God will answer. It comes down to self-awareness and seeing what everyone else already sees.

2. **Seek His Face**. Consistency is what He's looking for. You have to stay before Him until discipline becomes desire. The more you seek Him, the hungrier you become. That's when you know you're truly seeking His face. You can't pursue wickedness and seek His face at the same time. When you pursue Jesus, you will automatically turn from your wicked ways.

3. **When we do our part, He does His**. He opens the Heavens (literally) and brings what you need to earth. He comes to you with healing in His hands. I've experienced this so powerfully. You can, too!

Live Like God Intended

Read 2 Corinthians 5:17 in the Amplified translation:

> "Therefore, if anyone is in Christ [that is, grafted in, joined to Him by faith in Him as Savior], *he is* a new creature [reborn and renewed by the Holy Spirit]; the old things [the previous moral and spiritual condition] have passed away. Behold, new things have come [because spiritual awakening brings a new life]."

How has this truth impacted your decisions and choices?

_____

God is the only One who can give us a clean slate, a fresh start, a do-over, and a new beginning. We each must do our part, so *walk* in this newness of life, and then join with others to live as He intended.

Humbly Pray and Seek

If My people who are called by My name will humble themselves,
and pray and seek My face…
I will hear from heaven… and heal their land.

Our country is in desperate need of God's touch. You and I must gather with other believers who are called by His name and follow God's instructions to bring His healing to our land.

Don't wait another day!

Week 18, Day 6

HEARING & OBEYING GOD'S VOICE

REFLECTION QUESTIONS FOR YOU TO ANSWER THIS WEEK...

1. This week we learned God loves us for who we are, not for what we can or cannot do. His love for us is not performance-based. His perfect love sends fear running and invites freedom into our souls.

Did you grow up in a performance-based family atmosphere? _____

How has God's love freed you from that bondage?

_____

2. *What important lessons did you learn about your circumstances and God's truth?*

_____

_____

How has this impacted how you deal with the situations you have to face in your life?

_____

_____

_____

3. Our country is in desperate need of God's touch. *How have you answered God's call to bring healing to our city/country (land)?*

_____

_____

"Prayer honors God, acknowledges His being,
exalts His power, adores His providence,
secures His aid."

— E.M. Bounds[34]

"In order for the inner man to be strengthened
with power through the Holy Spirit,
the children of God must discharge their responsibility.
They need to yield specifically to the Lord, forsake
every doubtful aspect in their life,
be willing to obey fully God's will and believe through prayer
that He will flood their spirit with His power."

— Watchman Nee[35]

Today's Rhema Word – Week 19, Day 1

CHECK YOUR CONNECTION

"I am the sprouting vine and you're my branches.
As you live in union with me as your source,
fruitfulness will stream from within you—
but when you live separated from me you are powerless."
(Jesus in John 15:5 TPT)

If the toaster is not working, before I throw it out, I check to see if it's plugged in. I check the connection. If my lamp doesn't work, I check the connection. In the natural, when something doesn't work that requires electricity, we first check the connection. In the spiritual, the principle is the same. If there are areas in our life that aren't working, we have to check our connection to the power source. Jesus uses the illustration of a vine and a branch. Every branch is designed to grow fruit. It's part of its original design.

As sons and daughters, we are hard-wired to be fruitful in everything we do as long as we stay connected to our Father. Sometimes, we get the idea we can make things happen without Him. We can do some things without God, but then we must sustain them ourselves. Whatever He does, He sustains, and it becomes a blessing to us and all the others around us. We are designed to bear much fruit.

So, when life isn't quite working,
check your connection.

Learn From Jesus

In John 15:7, Jesus says when we have that type of connection, we can ask the Father and _____

_____

Live Like Jesus

He is a God of multiplication.

In Genesis 1:28, God told them to _____

2 Timothy 2:2 instructs us to _____

_____

Acts 12:24 says, _____

Love through Jesus (go and do)

What did Jesus do in Matthew 15:32-39? _____

_____

Why did He say He did it? _____

What did the disciples say in verse 33? _____

_____

Sometimes, we get the idea we can make things happen without Him. Whatever God does, He sustains, and it becomes a blessing to us and all the others around us.

Stay connected to your power source, go do what He is sending you to do with Him, and bear much fruit.

Today's Rhema Word – Week 19, Day 2

GOOD SEED, BAD SEED

"Most assuredly, I say to you, unless a grain of wheat falls into the ground and dies, it remains alone; but if it dies, it produces much grain. He who loves his life will lose it, and he who hates his life in this world will keep it for eternal life."
(Jesus in John 12:24-25 NKJV)

We understand that in order to live for Christ we must die to self. Not physically die, however, something has to move out of the way so the Holy Spirit can move in! He lives inside of us. The Holy Spirit will obey and carry out the will of the Father on the earth. There is only one problem. We get in the way. We know selfishness, rebellion, disobedience, lust, lying, greed, manipulation, fornication, sexual perversion, gossip, jealousy, fear, rejection, bitterness, contention, brokenness, anger, revenge, isolation, and covetousness must die.

All these things are like a seed. A seed always reproduces after its kind. Therefore, we must ask the Holy Spirit to help us put to death these bad seeds and replace them with good seeds.

Lust is replaced by love.

Lying is replaced by telling the truth

Anger is replaced with compassion.

Get out of His way. Let selfishness die!
Let Him live in you and through you for all to see!

219

Learn From Jesus

In Matthew 13:24-30, Jesus told a parable about good and bad seeds. Then He explained it to His disciples in verses 36-43.

Explain the good seed:

_____

_____

Explain the bad seed:

_____

_____

Why did Jesus say understanding this principle was so important?

_____

Live Like Jesus

Complete Galatians 6:7-8. "Do not be deceived: God cannot be _____. A man _____ what he _____. Whoever sows to please their _____, from the flesh will reap _____; whoever sows to please the _____, from the Spirit will reap _____ _____" (NIV).

Love through Jesus (go and do)

Read Galatians 6:9-10.

The Word of God is like a seed that must be planted and nourished in the hearts of others.

Boldly go and do as the Holy Spirit leads you.

CHANGED BY HIS LOVE

"And you shall love the LORD your God with all your heart, with all your soul, with all your mind, and with all your strength.' This is the first commandment. "And the second, like it, is this: 'You shall love your neighbor as yourself.' There is no other commandment greater than these."
(Jesus in Mark 12:30-31 NKJV)

According to Jesus, it seems the only way to truly be able to love people is to love ourselves, and the only way to love ourselves is to know the love of the Father. Until we allow the pure love of God to touch us and change us from the inside out, we are only capable of loving others through our brokenness and pain. Our love for others is broken and painful to them because it's jaded, inconsistent, and conditional. We don't love ourselves very much. Sometimes, we don't even like ourselves. We end up projecting our pain and unhappiness onto others.

However, when we allow the Father to go into the deep places of our hearts, heal and love us, then we are capable of loving others as we now love ourselves through our love relationship with Jesus.

Fall in love with Jesus. You will be changed by His love. Then loving others will come supernaturally.

Learn From Jesus

Ask Yourself…

How is my relationship with my family?

How is my relationship with my co-workers?

How do I get along with other Christians?

How is my relationship with myself?

According to Jesus, what is the only way to truly be able to love other people?

Love through Jesus (go and do)

Before you can go and love others through Jesus, you need to pray and ask the Father to work on you from the inside out.

Pray: *Father God, I love You with all my heart, all my soul, and all my mind. I ask Your pure love to go deep into my heart and touch me, heal me, and change me from the inside out, so I can become capable of loving others as You have commanded. I no longer want my love for others to be broken and painful to them because it's jaded, inconsistent, and conditional. Help me to see myself through Your love so I no longer project my pain and unhappiness onto others. Help me to love them as You love them and truly be a reflection of Your pure love through Jesus. Thank You, Father, for Your amazing love!*

Today's Rhema Word – Week 19, Day 4

GOD'S WORK IN AND THROUGH YOU

"Nevertheless do not rejoice in this,
that the spirits are subject to you,
but rather rejoice because your names are written in heaven."
(Jesus in Luke 10:20 NKJV)

Celebrating what God is doing **in us** is more important than what He does **through us**. Our greatest victories are not how powerfully God moves through us but how powerfully He moves inside of us. It's awesome for God to use us to minister life to someone. However, what we must cherish is when He ministers life to us. We are of no help to anyone if we ourselves remain broken.

The disciples had recently come back from powerful ministry experiences where God used them to do many miracles. Naturally, they were excited. It is exciting to be used by God. I ministered recently and saw people healed. I was stoked! However, the greater miracles are what He is doing inside of me. That is what gets me the most excited. In fact, the more He does in me, the more He wants to do through me.

Allow God to do a deeper work **in you**.

Then prepare to experience His miraculous works **through you** to others.

Learn From Other Bible Translations

J. B. Phillips, in the PHILLIPS Bible, says, "It is true that I have given you the power to tread on snakes and scorpions and to overcome all the enemy's power—there is nothing at all that can do you any harm. **Yet it is not your power over evil spirits which should give such joy, but the fact that your names are written in Heaven**" (emphasis added).

Eugene H. Peterson, in the Message Bible, says, "No one can put a hand on you. **All the same, the great triumph is not in your authority over evil, but in God's authority over you and presence with you. Not what you do for God but what God does for you—that's the agenda for rejoicing**" (MSG emphasis added).

Love through Jesus (go and do)

Allow God to do a deeper work **in you**. The more He does in you, the more He wants to do through you.

Document your amazing journey in writing and photos as you experience His miraculous works **through you** to others.

_____

_____

Today's Rhema Word – Week 19, Day 5

JOURNALING

So then you must perceive us—not as leaders of factions, but as servants of the Anointed One, those who have been entrusted with God's mysteries. The most important quality of one entrusted with such secrets is that they are faithful and trustworthy.
(1 Corinthians 4:1-2 TPT)

I've never been one who liked to journal, but over the past few years, I've learned an important principle. It's the principle of stewarding the mysteries of God. We are in a relationship with our Father which means we share back and forth. Us to Him and Him to us. When He communicates with us, everything He says has life contained in it. Nothing He says goes to waste.

Whether it's a vision, an impression, a word, a dream, or a gesture, it's all deep and rich with meaning. We may not understand everything He says, but it becomes our responsibility to steward all His communications. There have been times He says something I do not understand only to later discover the meaning. I can't rely on my memory to recall everything He says to me. When I write down what I hear or see, it lets Him know it matters to me. When He knows it matters to me, He wants to communicate more. My advice is that you create a place in a journal or on your phone to write down every time the Father comes to you. You will be amazed and blessed.

Journal the Mysteries of God

When God communicates with us, everything He says has life contained in it. Journaling will help you remember and better process what He shares with you. Record it whether it is:

A vision _____
_____

An impression _____
_____

A word_____
_____

A dream_____
_____

A gesture _____
_____

Other_____
_____

When it is revealed to you, record its deep, rich meaning. Include as many details as you can recall.

Journaling lets Him know what He gives you matters to you. When He knows it matters to you, He will want to continue communicating with you.

So, write down every time the Father comes to you.

You will be amazed and blessed.

Week 19, Day 6

HEARING & OBEYING GOD'S VOICE

REFLECTION QUESTIONS FOR YOU TO ANSWER THIS WEEK...

1. This week you learned when you live separated from your power source, you are powerless.

Explain why this principle has become so important in your life:

_____

_____

2. You also learned how a seed always reproduces after its kind.

What are the two kinds of seeds that can be planted in our hearts?

_____

_____

Where do these seeds come from?

_____

_____

3. *According to Jesus, what is the only way to truly be able to love others?*

_____

_____

4. Remember to write down every time the Father comes to you with a word, vision, or dream. You will be blessed!

"By grace I understand the favor of God, and also the gifts and working of his Spirit in us; as love, kindness, patience, obedience, mercifulness, despising of worldly things, peace, concord, and such like."

— William Tyndale[36]

"A spiritual gift is a supernaturally designed ability granted to every believer by which the Holy Spirit ministers to the body of Christ. A spiritual gift cannot be earned, pursued, or worked up. It is merely 'received' through the grace of God."

— John MacArthur[37]

Today's Rhema Word – Week 20, Day 1

UNLOCK THE SPIRITUAL REALM

I pray that the Father of glory, the God of our Lord Jesus Christ,
would impart to you the riches of the Spirit of wisdom and
the Spirit of revelation to know him
through your deepening intimacy with him.
I pray that the light of God will illuminate
the eyes of your imagination, flooding you with light, until
you experience the full revelation of the hope of his calling—
that is, the wealth of God's glorious inheritances
that he finds in us, his holy ones!
I pray that you will continually experience the immeasurable greatness
of God's power made available to you through faith. Then your lives
will be an advertisement of this immense power as it works through
you! This is the mighty power.
(Ephesians 1:17-19 TPT)

I f you can know Christ in the way Paul describes in this prayer, you will never be the same. I started years ago praying this passage over my life. Jesus has been faithful to come to me with greater wisdom and revelation about Himself. My natural and spiritual eyes have been opened to things I have never seen before. It's like something in the spiritual realm unlocked for me. You can experience this, too!

He is eternal and infinite and has allowed you to tap into His flow. Pray this over your life with a sincere heart and watch what He does.

Learn From the Apostle Paul

If you can know Christ in the way Paul describes in this prayer, you will never be the same.

Personalize this prayer daily:

Father God, please impart to me the riches of the Spirit of wisdom and the Spirit of revelation to know You through my deepening intimacy with You. In Jesus' name, I pray.

Record God's answer:

_____

_____

Pray for God's Revelation

Father God, I pray today that the light of Your presence will illuminate the eyes of my imagination, flooding me with light, until I experience the full revelation of the hope of Your calling on my life. In Jesus' name, I pray.

Record God's answer:

_____

_____

Pray, Then Go and Do

Father God, I pray I will continually experience the immeasurable greatness of Your power made available to me through my faith. Make my life an advertisement of Your immense power as it works through me! In Jesus' name, I pray.

Record your experiences:

_____

_____

Today's Rhema Word – Week 20, Day 2

GOD, THE ALL-KNOWING ONE

The fear of the LORD is the beginning of knowledge,
but fools despise wisdom and instruction.
(Proverbs 1:7 NKJV)

The first step in our journey with the Lord is to revere Him. He is omniscient (all-knowing). He wants us to get to know the All-Knowing One. The way He does that is by releasing wisdom to us. Wisdom is not smarts or intelligence. It's the ability to navigate and advance in life in a way that doesn't waste time and produces results for all to see. We can ask for wisdom and His Word says He gives it to us generously. We can also accept counsel from wise men and women.

One of the most annoying types of people is a know-it-all, opinionated person who knows everything, is closed to anything new, resents discipline, and refuses to learn. Solomon calls this kind of person a FOOL

Don't be a know-it-all. Instead, be open to the advice of others, especially those who know you well and can give valuable insight and counsel. Learn how to learn from others.

Remember, only God is All-Knowing One,
the only Know-It-All!

Learn How to Learn From Others

Be open to the advice of others, especially those who you respect, know you well, and can give valuable insight and counsel. They have lots of it to give away if you're willing to listen.

Who are those God is telling you to seek for valuable insight and counsel? [

_____

_____

Ask God for Wisdom

What does James 1:5-7 say about asking God for wisdom?

_____

_____

Use God's GPS, Then Go and Do

God's GPS gives you the ability to navigate and advance in life in a way that doesn't waste time and produces results for all to see.

Map out God's directions and then go and complete your assignment:

_____

_____

_____

_____

Today's Rhema Word – Week 20, Day 3

GOD'S HEART WORK

*But the LORD said to Samuel, "Do not look at his appearance
or at his physical stature, because I have refused him. For the LORD
does not see as man sees; for man looks at the outward appearance,
but the LORD looks at the heart."*
(1 Samuel 16:7 NKJV)

When God is selecting people for their assignments, it has nothing to do with the obvious. It's hard for us to see people as they are. All we have to go on is what they look like, how they behave, and what they say. God sees us totally differently. The prophet Samuel was looking for the next King. He missed him, and so did David's father. Two people who should have been aware of David's potential for the throne missed it. God doesn't miss anything.

It doesn't matter who you are or even where you are, God will find you. You can live in the most remote of places in total obscurity and He will find you. This is a great lesson because often the way we prepare ourselves for His service is based on external standards. We become concerned about being where we can be noticed and recognized for what we are doing. God is in search of those who are "heart training." Heart training is developing who you are when no one is looking. When it's just you alone.

God's Heart Training

David was kingly when no one was around to see or even care. He was passionate about God even when he was all by himself.

Where did David's heart training begin? _____

What prepared him to be king and write so many psalms?

_____

_____

What did Moses' heart training prepare him to do?

_____

_____

What did John the Baptist's heart training prepare him to do?

_____

_____

What did Paul's heart training prepare him to do?

_____

_____

God's heart training is developing who you are

when no one is looking. Your public ministry begins in private. Your worship life begins in your secret place. Your development begins away from the spotlight and the applause.

When it's time and you've passed His test, He sees you and will promote you. Don't forsake the heart training. When you're ready, it will make all the difference in the world. Then you can go and do publicly what He has prepared you for in private.

Today's Rhema Word – Week 20, Day 4

NO RISK, NO REWARD

So then faith comes by hearing,
and hearing by the word of God.
(Romans 10:17 NKJV)

Faith is developed by growing and developing your spiritual hearing through studying the Word of God. Spiritual hearing is your spirit picking up on the spiritual frequencies in the atmosphere. In other words, you can detect what is happening in the spiritual realm around you and what is in the heart of God to do something about it.

Spiritual hearing is developed by growing in the Word of God. Everything for life and the God lifestyle is contained in His Word. The more you know Him through the Scriptures by way of revelation (Ephesians 1:17) the clearer you will hear His voice.

Once you can hear His voice clearly, you will be willing to risk releasing what you are hearing from God into the natural realm. That's when miracles begin to happen. That's when the things around you have to conform to heaven's reality. That's when you become an agent and carrier of change and transformation everywhere you go.

No RISK, no REWARD.

Developing Spiritual Hearing

Our world uses radio waves to make our cell phones, garage door openers, and baby monitors function. Like these radio waves, God gives spiritual insights to keep us in tune with Holy Spirit so we can function in His service.

Read 1 Corinthians 2: 9-16.

How do you tune into God's divine frequency?

_____

_____

Live Like Jesus

*His **divine power** has given us everything we need....so that you may **participate in the divine nature**.* (NIV)

How has the promise in 2 Peter 1:3-4 helped you to detect what is going on in the spiritual realm?

_____

_____

Love Through Jesus (go and do)

Once you can hear His voice clearly, you'll be willing to risk releasing what you're hearing from God and miracles begin to happen. That's when you become an agent of change and transformation everywhere you go. *What are you sensing He is telling you to go and do?*

_____

_____

Today's Rhema Word – Week 20, Day 5

THE UNEXPECTED GIFT

A man's gift makes room for him,
And brings him before great men.
(Proverbs 18:16 NKJV)

When you really bless someone with a wonderful, unexpected gift, you have earned their favor. They are more willing to do anything for you. That's typically how it works in the natural.

There is a spiritual principle in play when the Holy Spirit manifests through you with one of His spiritual gifts. People will take notice. Suddenly, you go from obscurity to front and center. The gifts of the Holy Spirit demand attention (1 Corinthians 12:7-10). They demand a place to show the world God's love and power through you. Proverbs 18:16 says, "The *right* gift *at the right time* can open up new opportunities and gains access to influential people" (VOICE).

1 Corinthians 12:1 says, "Now about the spiritual *gifts* [the special endowments given by the Holy Spirit],…I do not want you to be uninformed" (AMP). Eagerly desire to manifest these spiritual gifts in your life. 1 Corinthians 12:7 says, "Each believer has received a gift that **manifests the Spirit's *power and presence.*** That gift is given for the **good of the whole community**" (VOICE).

Grow in them, God will take care of the rest.

Learn From the Holy Spirit

Proverbs 18:6 and 1 Corinthians 12:1-7 are obviously saying that we need to learn about and then operate in cooperation with the Holy Spirit to manifest the gifts as He directs. He doesn't want you to be uninformed.

As you read the list of the Gifts of the Spirit, which one(s) is He telling you to seek to grow in?

What have you learned by studying these gifts?

_____

_____

Live Like Jesus

There is a spiritual principle in play when the Holy Spirit manifests through you with one of His spiritual gifts. People will take notice.

As you have made yourself available to the Holy Spirit to manifest through you, what have you seen happen in others?

_____

_____

Love Through Jesus (go and do)

These gifts of the Holy Spirit demand a place to show the world God's love and power through you.

Continue to grow and learn and then go and do what He is directing.

Record in your journal how He has used you with the *right* gift *at the right time* and opened new opportunities and given you access to people of influence.

Week 20, Day 6

HEARING & OBEYING GOD'S VOICE

REFLECTION QUESTIONS FOR YOU TO ANSWER THIS WEEK...

1. This week you began by learning how to open your natural and spiritual eyes to things you have never seen before.

What happened when you prayed, "Make my life an advertisement of Your immense power as it works through me!"?

_____

_____

2. Once you can hear His voice clearly, you will be willing to risk releasing what you are hearing from God into the natural realm. That's when miracles begin to happen and things around you must conform to heaven's reality.

Share how you become an agent and carrier of change and transformation everywhere you went after learning to hear and respond to His voice.

_____

_____

3. "The *right* gift [spiritual gift] *at the right time* can open up new opportunities and gains access to influential people" (Proverbs 18:16 VOICE).

How have these new opportunities and access to influential people impacted your life and ministry?

_____

_____

"Enter into the promises of God. It is your inheritance. You will do more in one year if you are really filled with the Holy Ghost than you could do in fifty years apart from Him."

— Smith Wigglesworth[38]

"Without the Spirit of God we can do nothing. We are as ships without wind or chariots without steeds. Like branches without sap, we are withered. Like coals without fire, we are useless. As an offering without the sacrificial flame, we are unaccepted."

— Charles Spurgeon[39]

Today's Rhema Word – Week 21, Day 1

ENCOUNTER WITH THE HOLY SPIRIT

*"Then the Spirit of the LORD will come upon you, and you will prophesy
with them and be turned into another man. And let it be, when these signs
come to you, that you do as the occasion demands; for God is with you."*
(1 Samuel 10:6-7 NKJV)

Saul was a regular guy until he had his first encounter with Holy
Spirit. Once you encounter the Spirit of the Lord, you literally
become a different person. He frees you of a desire to sin. You become
the person He designed you to be. There is nothing better than having
an authentic encounter with the Lord. It's other worldly, mind-blowing,
and it wrecks you in a good way. It cannot be mistaken for something else.

The Father is waiting to encounter you and me. He wants to break
into our world and touch us. He sees our hearts for Him and desires
to come to us.

Ask the Father for an encounter with the Holy Spirit. Ask Him to
disrupt your world, your routine, and turn you into another man or
woman. He will.

I'm a witness, He's come to me in incredible ways. It changes everything in and around you. I pray in the name of Jesus Christ that the
Spirit of the living God comes to you now.

Learn From Saul and Peter

What happened to Saul in 1 Samuel 10:9-11 after the Spirit of God came upon him?

_____

_____

What happened to Peter in Acts 2:14-41 after the Holy Spirit came upon him?

_____

_____

Encounter with the Holy Spirit

Ask the Father for an encounter with the Holy Spirit.

What happened when God answered your prayer?

_____

_____

How has God disrupted your world?

_____

_____

_____

How has He disrupted your routine?

_____

_____

Describe how He turned you into another man or woman.

_____

_____

Today's Rhema Word – Week 21, Day 2

BAPTIZED WITH THE HOLY SPIRIT

"Then I remembered the word of the Lord, how He said,
'John indeed baptized with water,
but you shall be baptized with the Holy Spirit.'"
(Peter in Acts 11:16 NKJV)

S ome close friends told me about the baptism of the Holy Spirit. "I haven't experienced that," I thought. "If that's something for all believers, I don't want to be left out." I started reading books and searching the Scriptures. I concluded it was for me and began to pray every day for God to cleanse me and baptize me with His Holy Spirit.

I prayed for months, and nothing happened. One evening, I was in bed not quite asleep, and I felt a rumbling like a volcano was about to erupt in my innermost being that moved upward toward my mouth. When it reached my mouth, I clinched my lips and like a balloon my cheeks were filled with air until the sensation subsided. Then it happened again just minutes later. I was in total awe and knew it was supernatural.

Two days later, I was at home alone worshipping, when in the midst of my singing, I began to speak in another tongue. I didn't understand what I was saying, but I knew it was from the Holy Spirit. Needless to say, my spiritual life radically changed from that point forward. A boldness and spiritual power were newly in me.

Seek, ask, and knock.
The door to the glorious life in the Spirit awaits you.

Learn From Jesus

Peter was referring to Jesus' instructions to them in Acts 1:4-5.
How was the baptism of the Holy Spirit described in Acts 2:1-4?

_____

_____

What happened to the disciples after they experienced this?

_____

_____

Live Like a Disciple of Jesus

In Acts 1:8, why did Jesus say His disciples needed to wait for the baptism of the Holy Spirit?

_____

_____

Love Through Jesus (go and do)

As you studied the Acts of the Apostles in Chapters 1-8, what did you learn the Holy Spirit did through them after they were baptized by the Holy Spirit?

_____

_____

What do you need to do to add power to your ministry for Him?

_____

_____

Today's Rhema Word – Week 21, Day 3

TEACHING US TO WALK

You've gone into my future to prepare the way,
and in kindness you follow behind me
to spare me from the harm of my past.
With your hand of love upon my life,
you impart a blessing to me.
(Psalm 139:5 TPT)

When God created us, He already had our purpose established. His love for us calls us into our destiny. He literally stands in the future where our purpose is fully realized, and from a distance calls us to come to Him. It's like a father who teaches his son or daughter how to walk. He stands them up, runs ahead of them, and calls them to come. Their face lights up with laughter and giggles as they stumble their way to the father. They fall occasionally, but he runs, lifts them up, and goes back to call them to himself.

So it is with our Heavenly Father. He's not just walking alongside us saying, "You can do it." He's already at our destiny calling us to it. He protects us along the way, though not shielding us from the occasional bump or bruise. He assures us we can do it. He doesn't stop until we make it to Him.

Let's keep our eyes on Him with childlike hearts full of giggles. He's calling us into our destiny.

Learn From the Father

Father God stands in the future where our purpose is fully realized and from a distance calls us to come to Him. Picture your Heavenly Father teaching you how to walk. His arms are open wide, encouraging you to keep moving forward toward your destiny.

What bumps have you experienced along the way?

_____

_____

How did Father God lift you up and put you back on the right path?

_____

_____

Keep Your Eyes On the Father

Read the Parable of the Prodigal Son in Luke 15:11-32. Picture the son in a pig pen, filthy and hungry.

Now, picture him approaching his father's house.

When he looks down the driveway, what does he see?

_____

_____

Don't Stop

He's assuring you that you can do it. He won't stop until you make it to Him. So, don't stop. Your destiny is waiting!

Declare:

He's gone into my future to prepare the way.

His hand of love is upon my life, teaching me to walk.

Today's Rhema Word – Week 21, Day 4

THE TRANSFORMING POWER OF THE GOSPEL

Beloved friends, what should be our proper response to God's mar-
velous mercies? I encourage you to surrender yourselves to God to be
his sacred, living sacrifices. And live in holiness, experiencing all that
delights his heart. For this becomes your genuine expression of worship.
Stop imitating the ideals and opinions of the culture around you but be
*inwardly **transformed** by the Holy Spirit through a total **reformation***
*of how you **think**. This will empower you to discern God's will as you*
live a beautiful life, satisfying and perfect in his eyes.
(Romans 12:1-2 TPT emphasis added)

When we walk in daily intimacy with the Holy Spirit, our soul—mind, will, and emotions—are in full submission to God's Spirit. Suddenly, we can discern the thoughts of God. The Scriptures call it having the "mind of Christ" (1 Corinthians 2:16).

This is the beginning of a brand-new world, the world that we are reborn into called Heaven. Now, our job is to bring Heaven to earth until where we are looks like where we're from.

Jesus said we should daily pray, "Your kingdom come, your will be done on earth as it is in heaven" (Matthew 6:10 NIV).

Learn From the Holy Spirit

What does it mean to be "inwardly transformed by the Holy Spirit through a total reformation of how you think"?

_____

_____

Ask yourself…

Is my mind, my intellect, will, and emotions (soul), in full submission to God's Spirit? _____

What changes need to be made in my life to correct my thinking?

_____

_____

Pray Like Jesus Taught

"Your kingdom come, your will be done on earth as it is in heaven" (Matthew 6:10 NIV).

What do you need to do to partner with the Holy Spirit to bring Heaven to earth?

_____

_____

Love Through Jesus (go and do)

Your mind is like a computer. The Holy Spirit uploads the software to give you the mind of Christ and rewrites your hard drive. "This will empower you to discern God's will as you live a beautiful life, satisfying and perfect in his eyes." Invite Him in!

Today's Rhema Word – Week 21, Day 5

TIMES OF TESTING

All the tests they endured on their way through the wilderness are a symbolic picture, an example that provides us with a warning so that we can learn from what they experienced. For we live in a time when the purpose of all the ages past is now completing its goal within us. So beware if you think it could never happen to you, lest your pride becomes your downfall. We all experience times of testing, which is normal for every human being. But God will be faithful to you. He will screen and filter the severity, nature, and timing of every test or trial you face so that you can bear it. And each test is an opportunity to trust him more, for along with every trial God has provided for you a way of escape that will bring you out of it victoriously."
(1 Corinthians 10:11-13 TPT)

God has provided you with a way of escape that will bring you out of any trial victoriously. He has shown you the good, bad, and ugly of all His sons and daughters in His Word. He didn't hold anything back because He wanted you to be aware of your journey ahead in Him. Temptation is not sin. It just means the enemy is hot on your trail because you have something very valuable that he wants. Don't be prideful and think you can handle him on your own. If you stay in the presence of the Holy Spirit, you will **always** see the exit sign He provides when the enemy begins harassing you. When the enemy realizes you won't fall for his old tricks anymore, he moves on. Resist him and he will flee.

Learn From Your Ancestors

Deuteronomy 8:2 reminds us to remember how God led them _____ the wilderness to _____ them. He did _____ take them _____ of the wilderness.

How should you pray when you are in the midst of a trial?

_____

_____

Defeat the Devil Like Jesus

Jesus had His own wilderness experience as recorded in Matthew 4:1-11.

How did Jesus defeat the devil's temptation attempts?

_____

_____

Resist the Devil, Then Go and Do

If you stay in the presence of the Holy Spirit, you will **always** see the exit sign He provides when the enemy begins harassing you. When the enemy realizes you won't fall for his old tricks anymore, he moves on.

Resist him and he will have to flee (see James 4:7).

Prepare a three-minute testimony of how this principle has been proven in your life.

Week 21, Day 6

HEARING & OBEYING GOD'S VOICE

REFLECTION QUESTIONS FOR YOU TO ANSWER THIS WEEK...

1. This week, you learned the importance of having the Holy Spirit operating in your life.

    Have you had a personal encounter with the Holy Spirit? ___

    How has that changed your life for the better?

    _____
    _____
    _____

2. You also read some stories in the Bible concerning the trials many of our ancestors encountered along their journeys with God.

    How have these stories helped you face your own trials?

    _____
    _____
    _____

3. 1 Corinthians 2:16 says we have the "mind of Christ."

    Describe what you now understand this means:

    _____
    _____
    _____

"Prayer is a sincere, sensible, affectionate pouring out of the soul to God, through Christ, in the strength and assistance of the Spirit, for such things as God has promised."

— John Bunyan[40]

"The Spirit-filled life is not a special, deluxe edition of Christianity. It is part and parcel of the total plan of God for His people."

— A. W. Tozer[41]

Today's Rhema Word – Week 22, Day 1

ENCOUNTER WITH JESUS

Look at you, my dearest darling, you are so lovely!
You are beauty itself to me.
Your passionate eyes are like gentle doves.
(Song of Solomon 1:15 TPT)

Because of the narrow shape of their head, a dove can only focus on one object at a time and always has a singular focus.

At a weekend encounter retreat for men, the minister told us to ask God for a revelation of the Cross. As I prayed with my eyes closed, in the far distance I could see a tiny light moving toward me. As it came closer, the light began to get bigger, and I could make out the face of Jesus in the light. His face came closer and closer until we were face-to-face. I thought I was looking at a picture of Jesus from my imagination. Then, to my surprise His eyes opened. As our eyes made contact, a warmth rushed through my entire body. I called it liquid love. Tears streamed down my face. It wasn't a static image from memory. It was Jesus! For that moment, I had one singular focus.

The dove represents the Holy Spirit who is calling us to a singular focus on Him and Him only. I pray Jesus will meet you in a tangible, real, life-changing way. I pray the fruit of your encounter will be a singular focus on the presence and person of the Holy Spirit for the rest of your life.

Learn From Jesus

What two things happened after Jesus was baptized by John in Matthew 3:13-17 before He began His ministry?

_____

_____

Live Like a Disciple of Jesus

Read Matthew 4:18-20. The first two men Jesus called to be His disciples must have had a face-to-face encounter with Jesus.

What did Jesus say to them?

_____

_____

How did they respond?

_____

_____

Read Matthew 4:21-22.

How did James and John respond to Jesus?

_____

_____

What is the key word in the disciples' responses to their encounters with Jesus? _____

Love Through Jesus (go and do)

Pray for a personal, face-to-face encounter with Jesus and immediately set your focus on following Him.

Today's Rhema Word – Week 22, Day 2

OUR FATHER'S EYE

I will instruct you and teach you in the way you should go;
I will guide you with My eye. (Psalm 32:8 NKJV)

When my sons were toddlers and beginning to walk and do various things on their own, their learning started with their mother and me teaching them. They would look intently into our eyes. Along with what we were teaching them, our eyes would make sweeping gestures that corresponded with what they were being taught. It didn't take long before all we had to do is look at them and we could direct them from a distance. There was a connection we had that went beyond the physical. It was relational. It was trust and confidence that we would never let them down or harm them.

Our Father in Heaven guides us with His eye. He gazes intently upon us. He never looks away. In turn, we look Him in His eye, gazing intently and never looking away. With the slightest of gestures, His eyes move, and we follow. We trust Him! In fact, we have become interdependent. We need Him and He desires us. We are relationally connected. The Father and I have now become one, I in Him and He in me. What an amazing life that we can be directed by the slightest movement of our Heavenly Father's eye. What an amazing life we have in Him.

Learn From Jesus' Prayer

In John 17:20-23, Jesus prayed for all believers.

He said, "I pray...that **all** of them may be _____, Father, just as _____ are in _____ and ____ am in _____. May they also be in ____...." (NIV).

We are relationally connected. What an amazing life we have in Him.

Live Like a Disciple of Jesus

1 Peter 3:12 says the eyes of the Lord are

_____

_____

Proverbs 15:3 says the eyes of the Lord are

_____

_____

2 Chronicles 16:9 says the eyes of the Lord are

_____

_____

Love Through Jesus (go and do)

How has the amazing promise from God in Psalm 32:8 impacted your service and ministry in the Kingdom of God?

_____

_____

Today's Rhema Word – Week 22, Day 3

THE LIMITLESSNESS OF THE HOLY SPIRIT

*The One whom God has sent to represent him will speak
the words of God, for God has poured out upon him the
fullness of the Holy Spirit without limitation.*
(John 3:34 TPT)

We have been given the Holy Spirit without measure. There is no limit to what the Holy Spirit can do in and through us. His first work is in us. We have to allow Him into every room of our soul. Nothing is off-limits. He can then do a deep cleaning.

One of the first things He does is rid us of selfishness. Selfishness is at the root of many of our troubles. Selfishness is wicked and it must go. It's not thinking less of yourself, it's thinking of yourself less. Then the Holy Spirit moves powerfully through us.

Your dreams and ambitions are probably too small. If you can accomplish your dream or ambition, it's too small. There must be a gap between where you are and what you dream, then He can fill that gap. There must be nervousness with the task, then He fills that gap and gives you confidence. There must be an impossibility staring you in the face, then He fills the gap because nothing is impossible for God.

Let's enjoy together the fruit of limitlessness as we watch what Holy Spirit was sent to this earth to do.

Allow the Holy Spirit to Work in You

The Holy Spirit works in you to rid you of selfishness.

What does a life look like when we prefer others above ourselves?

_____

What other areas is the Holy Spirit revealing He needs to work on in you?

_____

_____

Allow the Holy Spirit to Work Through You

There is no limit to what the Holy Spirit can do through you. Your dreams and ambitions are too small if you can accomplish them yourself. There must be an impossibility staring you in the face, then He steps in and fills the gap.

What "impossible" dreams and ambitions are staring you in the face?

_____

_____

Watch the Holy Spirit

Enjoy the fruit of limitlessness as you watch what the Holy Spirit was sent to this earth to do in and through you.

What are you seeing in your future through the limitless power of the Holy Spirit working in your life?

_____

_____

Today's Rhema Word – Week 22, Day 4

RIVERS OF LIVING WATER

On the last day, that great day of the feast, Jesus stood and cried out,
saying, "If anyone thirsts, let him come to Me and drink. He who
believes in Me, as the Scripture has said, out of his heart
will flow rivers of living water."
(John 7:37-38 NKJV)

Revelation shows us there is a river that flows from the Throne of God (Revelation 22:1). We would have to be nuts not to take Jesus up on His offer to come and drink of it. It has a promise and a challenge. The more we drink of the Spirit, the more He will flow from us. What we take in is not meant to stay. It's meant to give away. The degree to which we drink will determine the volume of living water that flows from our innermost being.

We know from the Word that the water that flows is for the healing of the nations (Revelation 22:2). That means all people groups. This is a real thing. It's something beyond what we can think or reason.

When we open our mouths (which is the primary release of the river that flows), those who are in the path of the river will experience the transforming power of Jesus literally washing over their lives and be changed forever.

Let's drink and drink and drink, and then…let it flow!

Learn From Jesus

What is the promise of John 7:37-38?

_____

_____

What is the challenge?

_____

_____

Love Through Jesus (go and do)

We know from Revelation 22:2 that the water that flows is for the healing of the nations. That means all people groups. Romans 10:14-15 asks us....

But how can they call on him to save them unless they believe in him?

And how can they believe in him if they have never heard about him?

And how can they hear about him unless someone tells them?

And how will anyone go and tell them without being sent? (NLT)

Romans 10:14-15 challenges all of us to open our mouths and release the river to flow over the lives of others with the transforming power of Jesus. Their lives will be changed forever as we go and do what He has called us to do.

Let's drink and drink and drink and then let it flow!

Today's Rhema Word – Week 22, Day 5

THE SUPERIOR REALITY

Set your mind on things above, not on things on the earth.
(Colossians 3:2 (NKJV)

Yes, feast on all the treasures of the heavenly realm
and fill your thoughts with heavenly realities,
and not with the distractions of the natural realm.
(Colossians 3:2 TPT)

The Heavenly realm and the natural realm are two different realities that overlap in our world. We are hard-wired by design to access the Heavenly realm. However, our default reality is the natural realm.

Consequently, most of our orientation and familiarity are with what our senses can detect and perceive. The problem with our default is that it is an inferior reality. Daily intimacy with our Father through the Holy Spirit gives us unlimited access to the Heavenly realm which is a **superior reality**. The more we pursue Heavenly things, the more the Heavenly realm will become real to us.

The goal is to tip the scales until all around us in the natural realm bows to a superior reality. It's costly! There is sacrifice required, but it's worth it. All of eternity for us and all those around us depend on it.

Let's go all in. You won't regret it.

Learn From Heavenly Realities

How acquainted are you with the Heavenly realm?

_____

_____

What stories can you share that speak to this reality?

_____

_____

Live Like a Disciple of Jesus

Picture a set of scales like the scales of justice. One side is the natural realm, the other is the Heavenly realm.

What do you need to do to tip the natural-realm side, so it bows to the superior reality of the Heavenly-realm side?

_____

_____

Daily intimacy with your Heavenly Father through the Holy Spirit gives you unlimited access to the Heavenly realm which is a **superior reality**.

Are you willing to make the sacrifice to tip the scales? _____

Remember all of eternity for you and all those around you is depending on you. It's time to go all in!

Week 22, Day 6

HEARING & OBEYING GOD'S VOICE

REFLECTION QUESTIONS FOR YOU TO ANSWER THIS WEEK...

1. This week, you were encouraged to seek a face-to-face **encounter with Jesus** and learned about the **Limitlessness of the Holy Spirit.**

How have these powerful lessons impacted your personal life and your ministry to others in His name?

_____

_____

2. *Romans 10:14-15 challenges all of us to do what?*

_____

_____

Why is it so important you pick up this challenge and go and do what He is telling you to do?

_____

_____

3. *As you pursued Heavenly things, did the Heavenly realm become more real to you?* _____

What are you now doing to tip the scales where all around you in the natural realm bows to a superior reality?

_____

_____

"As we trust God to give us wisdom for today›s decisions, He will lead us a step at a time into what He wants us to be doing in the future."

— Theodore Epp[42]

"The men who have done the most for God in this world have been early on their knees. He who fritters away the early morning, its opportunity and freshness, in other pursuits than seeking God, will make poor headway seeking Him the rest of the day. If God is not first in our thoughts and efforts in the morning, He will be in the last place the remainder of the day."

— E. M. Bounds[43]

Today's Rhema Word – Week 23, Day 1

GATES OF ENTRY

*"Evil originates from inside a person. Coming out of a human heart
are evil schemes, sexual immorality, theft, murder, adultery,
greed, wickedness, treachery, debauchery, jealousy, slander, arrogance,
and recklessness. All these corrupt things emerge from within
and constantly pollute a person."*
(Jesus in Mark 7:21-23 TPT)

Our goal in life is to live and love victoriously and powerfully as sons of our Father. It's to know Him and make Him known. However, there is a **real** war within us against our affections. Affections are the deepest most intimate connection to something. It's on the inside of us where our soul and spirit connect. It's clear by the Scripture that it's possible to contaminate or pollute our affections which immediately impacts our relationship with our Father.

How is it that we can become polluted from within?

How does pollution get inside?

We were created by God with sensory gates that are like doors to our soul and allow access through our eyes, ears, mouth, touch, imagination, etc. These are gates of entry designed by God so that we can completely be filled with wonder and His glory. We are in control of all access, but we need to be aware of the vulnerability of these gates.

265

Learn to Control Access

Read the Parable of the Pharisee and the Tax Collector in Luke 18:9-14. Do not lie to yourself like the Pharisee did saying he was not as bad as the tax collector.

Ask Yourself…

Is what I'm allowing access to bringing honor to Jesus?

Is He excited about what is marching through my gates?

Has there been any illegal entry through my sensory gates?

Evict all illegal polluting tenants!

Live Like a Disciple of Jesus

Read the powerful statement Jesus made in John 14:30. "I will not speak with you much longer, for the ruler of the world (Satan) is coming. **And he has no claim on Me [no power over Me nor anything that he can use against Me]**" (AMP).

Set your heart on things above, not on things below. Make sure you guard your sensory gates so Satan has no power or anything he can use against you!

Love Through Jesus (go and do)

Do what you were designed to do. When your affections are properly in place with the things of Heaven, you will know, and everyone looking at your life will know, too.

Today's Rhema Word – Week 23, Day 2

FROM ORDINARY TO EXTRAORDINARY

But God has chosen the foolish things of the world to put to shame
the wise, and God has chosen the weak things of the world to put to
shame the things which are mighty; and the base things of the world
and the things which are despised God has chosen, and the things
which are not, to bring to nothing the things that are,
that no flesh should glory in His presence.
(1 Corinthians 1:27-29 NKJV)

I've never considered the lifestyle I've chosen as foolish. I suppose from those who are looking at it from the outside it might seem strange or scary. I remember when I chose to leave the marketplace world of banking, people thought I was crazy! When I said I was moving my family to Puerto Rico, no one understood. When we stepped foot on the soil of Africa there were lots of concerns for our safety.

I have known no greater love than the love of my Father God other than the earthly love for my wife. In exchange for feeling and looking foolish, I have inherited His Kingdom and all its resources. I get to live a supernatural life in partnership with the King of Glory.

My ordinary life becomes extraordinary in His hands.

Learn From Jesus

Read the amazing truth Jesus revealed in Matthew 11:25, "I praise You, Father, Lord of heaven and earth [I openly and joyfully acknowledge Your great wisdom], that You have hidden these things [these spiritual truths] from the wise and intelligent and **revealed** them to infants [to new believers, to those seeking God's will and purpose]" (AMP).

What spiritual truth has God revealed to you as you seek His will and purpose for your life?

Live Like a Disciple of Jesus

What did the "spiritual leaders" say about Peter and John in Acts 4:13?

"Now the leaders were surprised and confused. They looked at Peter and John and realized they were *typical peasants*—uneducated, utterly ordinary fellows—with extraordinary confidence" (VOICE).

As an ordinary person, go and share God's truths with extraordinary confidence as you live a supernatural life in partnership with the King of Glory.

Today's Rhema Word – Week 23, Day 3

OFFER THE FIRST FRUIT OF YOUR DAY

O God, You are my God; Early will I seek You;
My soul thirsts for You; My flesh longs for You
In a dry and thirsty land where there is no water.
So I have looked for You in the sanctuary,
To see Your power and Your glory.
(Psalm 63:1-2 NKJV)

There definitely is a pattern in Scripture of a time to meet God. It is not a rule or a recipe for experiencing more of God. It simply says whatever you produce, give the first portion to the Lord in an act of gratitude and honor. I believe David was giving the first fruit of his time to the Father.

I also believe there is something about the stillness in the early morning when the world is not moving around that is conducive to meeting God. It has been my delight for over 20 years to rise early and meet with my Father and I have never lacked experiencing His glory and supernatural power.

Offer the first fruit of your day and spend it with your Heavenly Father. When you do, you will find everything about the rest of your day will be divinely guided.

Learn From David

Fill in what David says in these Psalms.

"In the _____, LORD, you hear my voice;

in the _____ I lay my requests before you and wait expectantly" (Psalm 5:3 NIV).

"Let the _____ bring me word of your unfailing _____, for I have put my _____ in you. Show me the way I should go, for to you I _____ my life. (Psalm 143:8 NIV)

Live Like a Disciple of Jesus

What is the example Jesus left for us in Mark 1:35?

_____

_____

Do you give God the first fruits of your time every day? _____

Have you found that everything about the rest of your day is divinely guided when you do? _____

Explain:

_____

_____

*How is your day different when you **do not** start out your day with your Heavenly Father?*

_____

_____

Today's Rhema Word – Week 23, Day 4

MEANINGFUL RELATIONSHIPS

Pursue love, and desire spiritual gifts,
but especially that you may prophesy.
(1 Corinthians 14:1 NKJV)

Everything we do in the Kingdom, and every spiritual gift we receive, is about one thing—love. Love is about relationships. It's about being connected to people you know and who know you. It's about being accountable to people who want to see the best in you. There is no life in Christ outside of the context of **real,** meaningful relationships.

The gifts and God's power are awesome, but without first developing a relational heart of love, Paul says it's like clanging cymbals in the ears of God. Paul challenges us to pursue real relationships, **then** desire the gifts.

Everything God does is relationally connected through a genuine heart of love and compassion toward our family, friends, and even strangers.

Do not neglect to extend hospitality to strangers [especially among
the family of believers—being friendly, cordial, and gracious,
sharing the comforts of your home and doing your part gener-
ously], for by this some have entertained angels without knowing it.
(Hebrews 13:2 AMP)

Learn From the Teachings of Paul

Love is about relationships. It's about being connected and accountable to people you know and who know you.

Who are some of the people in your life you are accountable to?

_____

_____

There is no life in Christ outside of the context of **real**, meaningful relationships.

Describe what having real, meaningful relationships mean to you:

_____

_____

Live Like a Disciple of Jesus

Read Matthew 25:31-45.

What is the lesson Jesus is teaching here about your relationship with others?

_____

_____

What did Jesus say in verse 45?

_____

_____

Love Through Jesus (go and do)

Meditate on Hebrews 13:2 today as you go through your day.

Today's Rhema Word – Week 23, Day 5

SEARCHING FOR WISDOM

My child, will you treasure my wisdom? Then, and only then, will you acquire it. And only if you accept my advice and hide it within will you succeed. So train your heart to listen when I speak and open your spirit wide to expand your discernment—then pass it on to your sons and daughters. Yes, cry out for comprehension and intercede for insight. For if you keep seeking it like a man would seek for sterling silver, searching in hidden places for cherished treasure, then you will discover the fear of the Lord and find the true knowledge of God. Wisdom is a gift from a generous God, and every word he speaks is full of revelation and becomes a fountain of understanding within you. For the Lord has a hidden storehouse of wisdom made accessible to his godly lovers. He becomes your personal bodyguard as you follow his ways, protecting and guarding you as you choose what is right. Then you will discover all that is just, proper, and fair, and be empowered to make the right decisions as you walk into your destiny. When wisdom wins your heart and revelation breaks in, true pleasure enters your soul. If you choose to follow good counsel, divine design will watch over you and understanding will protect you from making poor choices. It will rescue you from evil in disguise and from those who speak duplicities. For they have left the highway of holiness and walk in the ways of darkness. They take pleasure when evil prospers and thoroughly enjoy a lifestyle of sin. But they're walking on a path to nowhere, wandering away into deeper deception. Wisdom, the Way of the Pure Only wisdom can save you from the flattery of the promiscuous woman—she's such a smooth-talking seductress! She left her husband and has forgotten her wedding vows. You'll find her house on the road to hell, and all the men who go through her doors will never come back to the place they were—they will find nothing but desolation and

273

despair. Follow those who follow wisdom and stay on the right path. For all my godly lovers will enjoy life to the fullest and will inherit their destinies. But the treacherous ones who love darkness will not only lose all they could have had, they will lose even their own souls! (Proverbs 2 TPT)

When I was in seminary, the professor taught us how to read the book of Proverbs with greater understanding. He introduced us to two characters in Proverbs that are central to the book—Lady Wisdom and Madam Folly. Folly means foolish. Proverbs is essentially a book written by Solomon to his sons. When you read Proverbs always look for Lady Wisdom and Madam Folly. I pray you will fall deeply in love with Lady Wisdom, and she will guide you all the days of your life.

Learn from Lady Wisdom

My child, will you treasure my wisdom? _____

Will you train your heart to listen when I speak and open your spirit wide to expand your discernment—then pass it on to your sons and daughters? _____

Highlight and meditate on the key verses from Lady Wisdom and accept her advice.

Week 23, Day 6

HEARING & OBEYING GOD'S VOICE

REFLECTION QUESTIONS FOR YOU TO ANSWER THIS WEEK...

1. This week, you learned from Lady Wisdom to *"train your heart to listen when I speak and open your spirit wide to expand your discernment—then pass it on to your sons and daughters."*

How has Lady Wisdom impacted you and your family's lives?

_____

_____

2. You also learned to set your heart on things above not on things below and to guard your sensory gates so Satan has no power or anything he can use against you!

Why is this so important to you and your ability to minister as a disciple of Jesus?

_____

_____

3. *Did you find that offering the first fruit of your day and spending it with your Heavenly Father made everything about the rest of your day divinely guided?*

Record in your journal how this has made a difference in your day-to-day life.

Make sure you share this truth with your children and watch it impact the next generation!

"Do you often feel like parched ground, unable to produce anything worthwhile? I do.

When I am in need of refreshment,
it isn't easy to think of the needs of others.
But I have found that if, instead of praying for my own comfort and satisfaction, I ask the Lord to enable me to give to others, an amazing thing often happens - I find my own needs wonderfully met.
Refreshment comes in ways I would never have thought of,
both for others, and then,
incidentally, for myself."

— Elisabeth Elliot[44]

Today's Rhema Word – Week 24, Day 1

FREELY RECEIVED, FREELY GIVE

"Heal the sick, cleanse the lepers, raise the dead,
cast out demons. Freely you have received, freely give."
(Jesus in Matthew 10:8 NKJV)

Lisa and I were at a worship event when the host of the evening said we can begin to pray for people who needed healing in their bodies. A woman seated next to us raised her hand. She explained she had been to the emergency room because the pain in her knee and shoulder was so bad. I laid my hand directly on the areas of pain and commanded them to leave. After a 15-second prayer, she moved both her knee and shoulder and said she could feel something happening, but there was still pain. I repeated the prayer two more times. The last time she said she felt a lot of heat coming from my hand. I felt it also. My whole body was hot and my head started sweating. Then, she said she heard three pops in her shoulder. She stood up and tested her knee and shoulder and proclaimed both were healed and pain-free. We praised the Lord!

Freely we have received, freely we give. It's wonderful to partner with Holy Spirit.

Learn From Jesus

Jesus was very clear with His instructions to His disciples and to us in Matthew 10:8.

What did Jesus say in...

Luke 9:1 _____

Mark 16:17-18 _____

John 14:12 _____

Live Like a Disciple of Jesus

We need to realize that if Jesus told us to do these things, He has given us the power and authority to do them. It's wonderful to partner with the Holy Spirit.

Describe an experience you had partnering with the Holy Spirit to give out of what He has given you to help others.

_____

_____

Love Through Jesus (go and do)

Pray and ask God to give you opportunities daily to freely give out of what He has given you the power and authority to do in Jesus' name.

Record in your journal each of your experiences.

Today's Rhema Word – Week 24, Day 2

FREEDOM OF CHOICE, BUT...

It's true that our freedom allows us to do anything, but that doesn't mean that everything we do is good for us. I'm free to do as I choose, but I choose to never be enslaved to anything.
(1 Corinthians 6:12 TPT)

You say, "Under grace, there are no rules and we're free to do anything we please." Not exactly. Because not everything promotes growth in others. Your slogan, "We're allowed to do anything we choose," may be true—but not everything causes the spiritual advancement of others. So don't always seek what is best for you at the expense of another.
(1 Corinthians 10:23-24 TPT)

The Apostle Paul is addressing what has been referred to as "hyper-grace." Romans 6:15 says, "So since we're out from under the old tyranny, does that mean we can live any old way we want? Since we're free in the freedom of God, can we do anything that comes to mind? Hardly. You know well enough from your own experience that there are some acts of so-called freedom that destroy freedom. Offer yourselves to sin, for instance, and it's your last free act. But offer yourselves to the ways of God and the freedom never quits" (MSG).

Learn From the Apostle Paul

"...but not everything causes the spiritual advancement of others. So don't always seek what is best for you at the expense of another."

The key message here from Paul is the effect our actions have on others, especially those we are attempting to witness to about Jesus.

What has the Holy Spirit revealed that you need to change so your witness is beneficial to others?

_____

_____

Live Like a Disciple of Jesus

Ask Yourself...

Is what I am doing going to build up my neighbor? _____

Will it show others I am a disciple of Jesus? _____

If not, what do you need to improve on?

_____

_____

Love Through Jesus (go and do)

"Beyond all these things put on and wrap yourselves in [unselfish] love, which is the perfect bond of unity [for everything is bound together in agreement when each one seeks the best for others" (Colossians 3:14 AMP). Go and do as an equipped disciple of Jesus!

Today's Rhema Word – Week 24, Day 3

GOD'S PEACE

And the peace of God, which surpasses all understanding, will guard your hearts and minds through Christ Jesus. (Philippians 4:7 (NKJV)

For He, Himself is our peace.... (Ephesians 2:14 a)

The Amplified Translations of Philippians 4:7 says,

"And the **peace of God** [that **peace** which reassures the heart, that **peace**] which transcends all understanding, [that **peace** which] stands guard over your hearts and your minds in Christ Jesus [is yours]" (emphasis added).

When things in life seem to be overwhelming and confusing, remember God promises us His peace to reassure our hearts. His peace is like a Guard standing watch over our hearts and minds, not permitting any illegal entry—God-honoring access only.

Remember, peace is not the absence of something; it's the presence of SOMEONE!

Christ himself is our peace. (Ephesians 2:14 a NIRV)

**Picture yourself as a lighthouse of peace filled
with the presence of Christ Jesus!
Receive the Peace of God Through Christ**

Declare Philippians 4:7 over your life:

The **peace of God** reassures my heart.

The **peace of God** transcends all understanding. The **peace** of God stands guard over my heart and mind in Christ Jesus.

I receive this **peace** in my life.

Live Like a Disciple of Jesus

Others will see this peace reflected in my life and seek it for their own lives.

Father God, may I be a lighthouse of Your peace in my neighborhood, at my job or in my school, and to my friends and relatives. May they see this wonderful peace You have given me through Christ Jesus and desire to know You. Guide me to those who need Your peace in their lives. In Jesus' name I pray.

Love Through Jesus (go and do)

"You are the light of [Christ to] the world" (Matthew 5:14 AMP).

"Let your light so shine before men, that they may see your good works and glorify your Father in heaven" (Matthew 5:16 NKJV).

Today's Rhema Word – Week 24, Day 4

CHOICES, CHOICES

"If you do what is right, will you not be accepted? But if you do not do what is right, sin is crouching at your door; it desires to have you, but you must master it." (Genesis 4:7 NIV)

1. Sin degrades and humiliates (the shameful reproach is never worth the sinful release.)

2. Sin steals joy (Nehemiah 8:10, Psalm 16:11, Proverbs 17:22,18:14). Joy is the most unmistakable sign of the presence of God.

3. Sin hurts Jesus (We wound the Savior, we spit in His face, we make a mockery of His love).

4. Sin hurts the sinner (Sin destroys a human life).

5. Sin hurts your family and friends (Joshua 7-Achan).

6. Sin steals time (Wasted time can never be regained. There's the actual time you sin when you could have done something better, then the time taken to get your relationship right with God again, time lost battling that sin over and over again with an open door.)

7. Sin is highly contagious. (Those around you can be infected like a disease that spreads.)

It comes down to choices. You get to choose.

Choose His life. Even though we fail, we are not failures.

Learn From Your Heavenly Father

How does God address us when we fail?

John 3:17 says, "For God did not send the Son into the world to **judge and** _____ the world [that is, to initiate the final judgment of the world], but that the world might be _____ through Him" (AMP).

God says, "I will not _____ you."

Isaiah 49:15 says, "Can a woman forget her nursing child, and not have compassion on the son of her womb? Surely they may forget, Yet I will _____ _____ you" (NKJV).

God says, "I will _____ _____ you."

God has said, "Never will I _____ you; never will I _____ you" (Hebrews 13:5 NIV).

Jeremiah 31:3 says, "Yes, I have loved you with an _____ _____; Therefore with lovingkindness I have drawn you" (NKJV).

God says, "I will never _____ loving you."

Today's Rhema Word – Week 24, Day 5

COMFORTED TO COMFORT OTHERS

Praise be to the God and Father of our Lord Jesus Christ,
the Father of compassion and the God of all comfort,
*who comforts us in **all** our troubles,*
so that we can comfort those in any trouble
with the comfort we ourselves have received from God.
(2 Corinthians 1:3-4 NIV)

We like the first part of this passage, but often miss the importance of the second part. The truth is everything we receive from God is meant to be used to help others. Once we learn this powerful concept, God will continually pour His blessings and favor on us so they can flow out through us to minister to others in His name.

Read verse 4 in the Amplified Translation: "who comforts *and* encourages us in **every trouble** so that **we will be able to comfort** *and* **encourage** those who are in **any kind of trouble**, with the comfort with which we ourselves are comforted by God" (emphasis added).

When God says all and every, He means all and every!

Remember, we are called to be His loving, comforting hands here on the earth when our fellow human beings are in **any and all** kinds of trouble!

Love Through Jesus (go and do)

Think about how you would like to be comforted during times of trouble in your life.

_____

_____

_____

When God sends His representative to comfort you, be thankful and then realize you are to do the same for another.

What are some ways you can comfort others?

_____

_____

_____

"Not one ounce of your grief, hurt, or loss will ever be wasted. God will redeem every teardrop. One way He will do this is by granting you the privilege of being a conduit for His comfort. God's comfort is meant to be transferred." – Paul Tautges with Joni Eareckson Tada

Week 24, Day 6

HEARING & OBEYING GOD'S VOICE

REFLECTION QUESTIONS FOR YOU TO ANSWER THIS WEEK...

1. This week, you studied how God has blessed you to be a blessing to others.

   How did Colossians 3:14 impact your life this week?

   _____

   _____

2. You were also challenged to picture yourself as a lighthouse of peace filled with the presence of Christ Jesus!

   How did you implement Matthew 5:14 and 16 in your life this week?

   _____

3. God comforts you to then go and comfort others like you have been comforted. This is God's heart for all of His children as they minister for Him throughout His kingdom.

Remember, you are called to be His loving, comforting hands here on the earth when our fellow human beings are in **any and all** kinds of trouble!

Final Word

What's Next?

I n the summer of 1983, I had my first "God encounter." I suffered a motorcycle accident, but one very different than normal. It was a late, dark evening when I was riding down a back street to my home. Speeding through an intersection, I was hit by a truck. Immediately, I heard God speak with detailed instructions on how I could survive the accident. At the moment of impact everything slowed down, as if I were watching a movie in slow motion. God then asked me a question, *"Do you want to live?"* I responded, "YES!" He then said, *"Grab the truck's bumper so you don't go the way of your motorcycle."* My motorcycle went under the truck and was completely mangled. Next, God said "Tuck your chin to your chest so your head doesn't bang against the concrete." The last words I remember hearing were, "Pray the truck doesn't run into anything." The truck then rolled to a stop. The entire incident took only seconds, and I was alive. ***It was a miracle!***

That word from God would be the first of many "Kingdom moments" I would have in the coming years. I can recall often hearing the voice of the Holy Spirit as if He were sitting on my shoulder. "He would point out people He wanted me to talk to or specific things He wanted me to do for Him." I always try to remember the secret to experiencing God's miracles. It's simple: "Listen to His voice and do what He says." Jesus is dying to reveal himself to his sons and daughters in His great redemptive plan to reach a world still waiting to be found.

Are you hungry for a fresh encounter with God? Do you long to hear His voice? Have you ever read through the gospels and the book of Acts and thought to yourself, "I want my life to look like the life of Jesus?" I have good news for you, it can!

Kingdom Moments has walked you through a daily journey of learning from Jesus and receiving His revelations from the Word of God. Living for Jesus and watching Him has demonstrated what it looks like to live out Kingdom principles. Loving through Jesus and receiving impartation and activation to see His Kingdom come alive in you. You have experienced a taste of the power, presence, and personal revival that Jesus brought to the world.

In the Scriptures, we see God speaking to His people in many different ways:

- Through dreams and visions, like God gave to Joseph or John the Apostle.

- In a direct way, like the moment God spoke directly from Heaven saying that Jesus was His beloved Son.

- Through prophets, like Isaiah, Amos, and Samuel.

- When people were praying to and worshipping God, like at Mt. Sinai or to Solomon when he asked God for wisdom.

- Through the gifts of the Holy Spirit, like wisdom, knowledge, and discernment.

- In *Kairos* moments, like the Exodus, the Ascension and Resurrection, as well as at Pentecost.

- Through the reading and study of the Scriptures.

- Even through a donkey! (Numbers 22:21-39)

Here is my question for you…**Are you hungry for more of God's presence and to hear His voice clearly. Are you always seeking, asking, and knocking?**

Kingdom Moments has begun to sharpen your ability to hear God's voice. Through faith and obedience, you will experience His supernatural life in all of life. Every day is filled with miracles. I encourage you to invest yourself in this devotional study again by adding fasting for the next six months. This second time, go through the book again to review your written interactions and to examine yourself for discipline and spiritual growth, as well as recommitting to thoughts, behaviors, and feelings that need to be strengthened in the truth of God's Word.

Ask the Holy Spirit to speak to you uniquely through this study. Just as the children of Israel followed God in a pillar of cloud by day, and a pillar fire by night. We read in Exodus 13:21-22, "By day the LORD went ahead of them in a pillar of cloud to guide them on their way and by night in a pillar of fire to give them light, so that they could travel by day or night. Neither the pillar of cloud by day nor the pillar of fire by night left its place in front of the people" (NIV).

Be sensitive and responsive to the leading of the Holy Spirit while going through *Kingdom Moments*. At times, He may ask you to pause and listen to His instructions. There may be times He prompts you to write a self-examination of where you used to be and how you have grown closer to Him. His goal is to be your guide throughout your faith journey with Him. Live continuously in His Kingdom Moments!

Endnotes

---

[1] *The Pursuit of God: The Human Thirst for the Divine*

[2] Quotes on God's Calling | Faith Unlocked (wordpress.com)

[3] www.christianquotes.info › a-w-tozer-quote

[4] www.christianquotes.info › a-w-tozer-quote

[5] www.christianquotes.info › a-w-tozer-quote

[6] www.liveatthewell.org › quotes-about-faith-and-trust

[7] Matthew 6:9-13

[8] Goodreads.com

[9] Goodreads.com

[10] Goodreads.com

[11] Goodreads.com

[12] Goodreads.com

[13] Dictionary.cambridge.org

[14] Goodreads.com

[15] goodreads.com

[16] Jean-Michel Hansen

[17] goodreads.com

[18] J.B. Phillips New Testament **(PHILLIPS)** The New Testament in Modern English by J.B Phillips copyright © 1960, 1972 J. B. Phillips. Administered by The Archbishops' Council of the Church of England. Used by Permission.

[19] Goodreads.com

[20] Goodreads.com

[21] Goodreads.com

[22] Goodreads.com

[23] Goodreads.com

[24] www.christianbook.com

[25] www.christianbook.com

[26] Leadership.org

[27] The Season of the Suddenlies - by James W. Goll - God Encounters

[28] Speedoftrust.com

[29] Goodreads.com

[30] Goodreads.com

[31] Goodreads.com

[32] Goodreads.com

[33] Goodreads.com

[34] Goodreads.com

[35] Goodreads.com

[36] Goodreads.com

[37] Goodreads.com

[38] Goodreads.com

[39] Goodreads.com

[40] Goodreads.com

[41] Goodreads.com

[42] Goodreads.com

[43] Goodreads.com

[44] Brainyquotes.com